Critical Guides to French Texts

55 Chrétien de Troyes: Yvain

Critical Guides to French Texts

EDITED BY ROGER LITTLE, WOLFGANG VAN EMDEN, DAVID WILLIAM

CHRÉTIEN DE TROYES

Yvain (Le Chevalier au Lion)

Tony Hunt

Reader in French,
University of St Andrews

Grant & Cutler Ltd
1986

© Grant & Cutler Ltd
1986
ISBN 0 7293 0239 3

I.S.B.N. 84-599-1103-9
DEPÓSITO LEGAL: V. 2.001 - 1985

Printed in Spain by
Artes Gráficas Soler, S.A., Valencia
for
GRANT & CUTLER LTD
11 BUCKINGHAM STREET, LONDON W.C.2

Contents

Contents

Preface

I have tried in the following pages to present a fresh, and to some extent unorthodox, interpretation of the *Yvain* and to turn aside from the well established views which are so repetitiously rehearsed in almost every new publication on Chrétien's romance and which can conveniently be identified from Douglas Kelly's bibliography (see our bibliography below) and from the pages of the annual *Bulletin bibliographique de la Société Internationale Arthurienne*. Consequently, the absence of references to many previous studies should not be taken as a mark of disdain or lack of appreciation on my part, but rather as a reluctantly accepted precaution in an attempt to secure the economy and effectiveness of my own arguments. All textual quotations are drawn from the edition of *Yvain* by T.B.W. Reid, which presents Foerster's text of 1912. As a former pupil of Reid I have taken particular pleasure in writing on a work in which he first stimulated my interest. I am grateful to Professor Wolfgang van Emden for his patience and encouragement, to my colleague Dr J. Supple for reading my first chapter, and to anonymous students at the University of Liverpool, who, through the kind offices of Dr Glyn Burgess, revealed to me that I had not always hit the right note in what is intended to be a student guide.

1. Twelfth-Century Romance

> Confound Romance! ... and all unseen
> Romance brought up the nine-fifteen.

Kipling's poem 'The King' (1894) is really no more successful in promoting the magic of modernity than Vigny's fundamentally backward-looking 'La Maison du Berger': both sadly confirm our reluctance to separate 'romance' from nostalgia, make-believe, retrospective idealism and adoring love. Yet none of these attitudes can legitimately be ascribed to Chrétien de Troyes. About Chrétien nothing is known except that he was very well known! His celebrity, however, is attested not by direct references to him, which are extremely rare, but by the number of romance writers who acknowledged his influence by reacting to his works — the incidents, themes, characters — in their own poems. In the thirteenth century, romance writing in France was dominated by the problem of coming to terms with Chrétien's achievement. Yet, if the literary figure of Chrétien is monumental, the historical figure is fleeting as a shadow. In *Le Chevalier de la charrete* (*Lancelot*) he tells us that he was writing at the instigation of that eminent daughter of a notorious mother, Marie de Champagne, child of Eleanor of Aquitaine (see McCash, *62*). Despite this authoritative information, Professor Benton has not been able to find a single historical record of a man called Chrétien at the court of Champagne (see *13*). Also by his own testimony, Chrétien wrote his religious grail romance, the *Conte du graal* (*Perceval*), for Philip of Alsace, but there is no evidence that he was ever at the court of Flanders (see Stanger, *79*). We do not know why this romance is unfinished. Chrétien de Troyes is simply a literary persona. The absence of a biography, whilst not problematic in itself, does leave us with the difficulty of determining when he composed his *œuvre* of five romances. Luttrell's recent attempt at a chronology, based on literary debts and influences, suggests 1184-90 as the period of composition of all his narrative works (see *60*: he is also credited with at least two lyrics and, in some quarters, with a 'hagiographical romance', *Guillaume d'Angleterre*). This is a decade later than the traditional dating which is still generally adhered to. There is common agreement that *Le Chevalier au lion* (hereafter *Yvain* for short) was written at the same time that Chrétien was working on the *Lancelot*, both romances being composed in several stages (between 1177-81, or, according to Luttrell, 1186-89). Whilst each of Chrétien's works was created in the spirit of an experiment, it is generally agreed that he was preoccupied with the implications of the Tristan story, the anti-social tenor of which he repudiated in favour of a more constructive role played by a 'héros civilisateur' (see Gallais, *38*).

In the twelfth century literary originality was identified with subtlety of interpretation and adaptation rather than with the creation of new subject matter. So far as can be discerned, all Chrétien's romances draw on already existing materials, notably motifs of Celtic origin assimilated to an essentially Latin culture. In the case of *Yvain* the figure of the 'lady of the fountain' bears a certain resemblance to features of a twelfth-century Latin life of St Kentigern (see Hunt, *55*, p.203). The Welsh prose tale (*chwedyl*) known as 'The Countess of the Fountain' (*Iarlles y Ffynnawn*) reproduces almost the entire story of Yvain (Owein), but in its surviving form it cannot be proved to be earlier than Chrétien and may, indeed, be dependent on him. It belongs, in any case, to a different milieu and a quite separate tradition of story-telling (see Hunt, *55*, pp.207ff.). Source study has, therefore, very little significance for the interpretation of *Yvain*.

From our ignorance of Chrétien the man and our uncertainty concerning the novelty of his materials it follows that our prime concern must be with the elucidation of the meaning of his work within the context of twelfth-century romance writing. In Chrétien's time the word *romanz*, as adverb, adjective and noun, signified the spoken vernacular as opposed to the more formal language of Latin. Indeed, it was sometimes used to indicate simply a spoken utterance, and, by extension, any composition, literary or technical, couched in a 'romance' i.e. continental French or Anglo-Norman, speech. In origin, therefore, *romanz* meant the linguistic medium of the illiterate, that is, of those who could not read or write Latin, and, by synecdoche, any work composed in that medium. These senses emerge in the context of a developing alternative culture to that of the Church, a culture which is not essentially serious, didactic and ecclesiastical, but imaginative, playful, and secular. The factors which promoted this secular culture are various: striking commercial expansion, growing urbanization, the rise of a money economy, a decrease in the popularity of celibacy, all reflected in demographic data. In particular, the flourishing schools of the eleventh and twelfth centuries led in northern France to a new spirit of enquiry and interrogation, the exegetical study of classical authors encouraged the humanistic discovery of the significance of the past, the rise of dialectic as a discipline produced a new sense of play (*lusus*) as a natural part of literary recreation, and *interpretation* came to be recognized as the prime activity of the cultivated mind (see Stock, *82*).

Innovations such as these find their expression in verse narratives composed of octosyllabic couplets designed to appeal to the courts' taste for refinement, luxury and the exotic, which exploited the metaphorical possibilities of such elements as expressions of moral truths (here the neo-platonism of writers associated with Chartres had an important part to play, see Wetherbee, *88*). Compositions of this kind have come to be known as romances and the quality of experience which they are thought to embody, however elusively, is often termed 'romance'. In other words, the expression *romance* indicates a language, a literary form, and a quality of experience. The latter, particularly hard to define, might be characterized as the temporary suspension of the laws of the real world to permit a vivid apprehension of the ideal. This often involves the acceptance of the strange, the fabulous or the unknown through the mediation of a love relationship which inspires and sustains the hero and which also encourages the reader to idealize too! The surface configurations of the romance are thus immediately appealing and attractive to the imagination, whilst at the same time embodying the metaphors and tensions which are problems to the critical mind. The romances can be read superficially for their decorative detail or more searchingly for their underlying implications and paradoxes. They constitute, after all, a response to the increase in lay patronage at the courts where the audiences included, on the one hand, the unlearned but leisured community of women with a desire for entertainment, and, on the other hand, a constantly expanding society of clerks, well educated, but either unsuccessful in their search for ecclesiastical preferment or anxious to remain in an essentially secular environment.

But the composition of the courts exercised a more precise influence on the nature of the romance. In an age largely indifferent to the rights of women, when the lot of the ladies at court was often perpetual neglect — the repudiation of wives was commonplace — it was inevitable that some element of compensatory idealism should be demanded of the romance and that the dissatisfaction generated by women's legal and economic dependence should be sublimated in an emotional hegemony whereby women were depicted as inspiring and directing reformed chivalric activity. In reality, we know, knightly *adventure* was military *adventurism*, chivalry was too often uncoordinated violence, destructive of friendships, families, and, in a still largely agrarian economy, of prosperity. Internecine squabbles, personal rivalry, the wholesale laying waste of others' lands, the primary role of looting and rapine in almost all military activity led to a social unease which the Church attempted to control through the peace movements and crusades (see below, pp.37ff.) and which lay authorities might hope to mitigate by 'socializing' knighthood through an association with women, refinement of manners, and moral justice — *les hommes font les lois, les femmes font les mœurs*. The elaboration of a distinctively 'knightly' life style became one of the major functions of the romance and may be seen as a projection of the nobility's desire for solidarity in the face of unwelcome pressure from the monarchy, on one side, and from the increasingly affluent bourgeoisie on the other. Such a social 'identity crisis' led to the adumbration of a chivalric ideal which smoothed away the socio-economic inequalities of the young knights or *juvenes* (see Duby, *29*) and substituted a unifying ethos which was largely an amalgam of moral precepts drawn from the works of Cicero and Christian spirituality. The contribution of the female and knightly components of court audiences to the ethical fabric of the romance was therefore considerable, but it was also complemented by the pretensions of the clerks, themselves often potential poets, who expected from the romance that same play of critical arguments in a fictional setting (*fabulosa narratio*) which they had found in the classical *auctores* and which the neo-platonism of Chartres had elevated to the essence of Christian poetry (see Wetherbee, *88*). The chivalric romance of the twelfth century thus associates *amor* and *chevalerie*, on the one hand, and *chevalerie* and *clergie* (learning), on the other.

The first of these two associations represents what is known as the chivalry topos (commonplace), which is an ethical circuit in which love of a lady inspires a knight to chivalric feats and endeavours, which in turn reinforce and promote the lady's love of him. The essence of the relationship is that the woman holds the dominant role of feudal lord, becoming the *dame*, *domina* or *dompna*, whilst the knight plays the part of her vassal (*hom*). It is this analogical extension of the feudal nexus to amatory relations which is the indispensable element of what is loosely, and perhaps unnecessarily, called 'Courtly Love' or *amour courtois* (see Boase, *16*). The romance's elevation of the lady and humbling of the knight have complex sociological ramifications which are a perpetual stimulus to reconsideration of the romance in the context of the historical conditions which produced it.

Equally important is the association of *chevalerie* and *clergie*, which forms part of another topos, called the 'transmission of learning' (*translatio studii*), a theme which finds its most succinct expression in the prologue to Chrétien's *Cligés* (see Hunt, *50*). There it is presented as the view that the schools of northern France have become the repository of ancient learning, not through antiquarian concerns, but by reason of a dynamic relationship with the ancient writers, above all the poets, as part of a humanistic conception of progress (see Hunt, *51*) which ultimately involves the harmonizing of pagan philosophy with

Christian theology in an effort of the imagination. *Interpretation* was therefore directed at uncovering and refining the sense (Old French *sen*) which was hidden by the poets within their works, lest, as Augustine explains in his *De doctrina christiana*, such works be cheapened by too facile an access. The concern of the schools with both practical explication (exegesis) and systematic interpretation (hermeneutics) leads in the romance to the literary *prise-de-conscience* of a new class of vernacular poets, excited by the possibilities of *literature*, understood not only in the normal twelfth-century sense of 'writing, the written word' and the sixteenth-century meaning of 'humane learning, wide reading, culture', but in the modern (eighteenth century onwards) sense of writing the significance of which derives not simply from *what is said* but from *the way it is said*. In this emergence of a literary self-consciousness Chrétien is a key figure, who appreciated the rich possibilities generated by the creation of multiple viewpoints — the poet (with his over-all view), the reciter (who may interpret the text through modulation of voice and gesture), the text's narrator or poetic persona, the fictional characters, and the multifarious members of the audience (see Green, *39*, and Scholz, *77*). What we have here is not the 'God's eye view' of a single-minded, omniscient creator, as in the nineteenth-century novel, but a multifocal presentation, exploiting irony, impersonation and a whole range of literary effects in constantly changing performances (often reflected in differences between manuscripts of the same work). Literature as *lusus* will occupy us throughout this study.

We have arrived at the notion of twelfth-century romance as a tale of chivalric love and adventure mediated by sophisticated literary devices in a multifocal presentation. Just as ironic or even parodic statements can be taken at face value by the less alert, so the romances might be superficially received as *aniles fabulae*, old wives' tales. Indeed, at the end of the twelfth century, or perhaps just a little later, a Latin poet wrote a satire in rhythmical verse on the absurdities, as he saw them, of the *Voyage de St Brendan*, which was composed early in the twelfth century and exhibits many similarities to courtly romance. In *Sir Thopas*, of course, Chaucer burlesques the romance, or at least the trivialized Middle English adaptations, and draws on himself the judgement of the host: 'Thy drasty ryming is nat worth a tord'. The progressive trivialization of the romance in ages which no longer operated the interpretative principles of the twelfth century was to lead to a strong reaction against the perceived 'vulgarity' of the genre, a reaction clearly detectable in Spain in the fifteenth century and all but universal in the Renaissance. The essential components of twelfth-century romance are, then, *amor*, *chevalerie* and *clergie*. It is now time to consider how these are combined and integrated in coherent narrative patterns and this brings us to the conventions of the romance as they were established in the twelfth century. The relative importance of these conventions is best distinguished by dividing them into three categories or strata, *characteristic* features, *distinctive* features, and *constitutive* features.

In the first category we include features which are characteristic of romance, but in no sense peculiar to it; sentimental relationships, deeds of valour, the happy ending (making the romance a 'comedy', in the medieval use of the word), the evocation of court life (including both *realia* and *exotica*), the aristocratic status of many of the characters, the prominence of women in the action. The combination of such features, all found separately elsewhere, represents in *Yvain* the backcloth against which more individualistic features are portrayed.

Distinctive features include the following: the isolation of the hero as 'un élu' responding to a vocation or calling; the idealized figure of the heroine; the appearance of Arthur (or an obvious substitute) as an authority figure; the trial or test which engages the hero's best energies; the elaboration of a distinctive topography. The latter quickly becomes familiar to the reader of romance, with the hero passing through a forest (Dante's *selva oscura*), along difficult paths ('per aspera ad astra'), reaching a crossroads (*bivium*), crossing bridges over rivers (water is an ubiquitous symbol), being exiled in a wilderness, receiving assistance from hospitable hosts and hermits, and relaxing in a beautiful, natural setting (*locus amoenus*) with its reminiscences of the Garden of Eden and the 'garden inclosed' (*hortus conclusus*) of the biblical *Song of Songs* (see Piehler, *71*; Thoss, *83*).

These motifs may support both psychological symbolism and Christian allegory, each setting constituting a kind of mental stage (*locus animae*) with special significance for the moral orientation of the hero. The distinctive topography of the romance is frequently reflected in medieval art and has an important structural function (see Boklund, *18*). It already, in a sense, presupposes the theme of the journey, the voyage, the pilgrimage (*peregrinatio*) undertaken by Man the Traveller (*homo viator*), the Pilgrim (*peregrinus*), the questing Knight (*chevalier errant*). It is here that we feel most strongly the influence of patristic and monastic writers who added to the metaphor of life's journey, involving education and evolution, the related images of the scale, step and ladder. In the romance the action is quite distinctively, therefore, located in the *quest* and the *gradus* or stages are represented by *adventures* which befall (*advenire*) the hero, rather than being provoked by him. This leads us to the essential dynamism of romance, the striking durability of which has often been linked with a pattern of events which rests on a psychological prototype variously identified as possession — loss — regaining of identity (Frye), departure — initiation — return (Campbell), or equilibrium — struggle — higher harmony (Hume) (for all these three see Hume, *48*). The search for an archetypal shape in romance has promisingly been linked to the psychic pattern known as *centro-version*, 'the gradual identification of the ego with the conscious rather than the unconscious' (see *48*, p.130) and the function of the marvellous interpreted as the reflex of psychic struggles, in other words as 'the physical world's equivalent to the unconscious in the mind'. Whilst this type of argument goes some way to explaining the perennial popularity of the romance, it does not account for the specific manifestations created by historical circumstances. It will be part of our argument in what follows to suggest that in the twelfth century in France elements of such psychic patterns are converted to a *game* made up of literary embodiments of contemporary fictions, notably the casuistry of courtly love and the ideology of knighthood.

In turning to the *constitutive* features of courtly romance, we must emphasize the necessity of confining our remarks to a clearly circumscribed cultural phase, namely the twelfth-century 'renaissance' in northern France. We have already emphasized the centrality of the *quest* in the dynamism of romance, a dynamism supported by the themes of *search* and *discovery* and reflected in a consistently interrogatory tone (questions, not affirmations, are the hallmark of romance rhetoric). If the romance is interrogatory, we may well ask to what its enquiries are directed. It is here that we encounter the greatest difficulty in defining the constitutive features of romance, for it is tempting to apply to the form as a whole statements which are truly valid only of the 'classic' or outstanding species of the genus, notably the works of Chrétien de Troyes, and particularly *Yvain*! It is partly a question of distributing the emphasis between the idealistic spirit of romance and its critical spirit. We have already seen that the experience labelled 'romance' involves the temporary suspension of the laws of the everyday world in favour of the claims of moral idealism mediated through love. It is natural to suggest that the recognition of these claims leads to the discovery and establishment of a new identity by the hero — a combination of the Delphic oracle's 'know thyself' and Polonius's 'To thine own self be true'. This view, for all its attractiveness, is more obviously applicable to the work of Chrétien than to the other romances. It receives support from the undoubted interest in the individual of many twelfth-century writers (see Hanning, *45* and Morris, *64*) and, particularly, of those who were intent on exploring the whole range of human love. In the romances the theme of identity is frequently externalized in the motifs of disguise, anonymity, use of pseudonyms (all found in *Yvain*!), but there is remarkably little explicit treatment of the inner life of the hero, and this is scarcely compensated for by the theory that the romances treat the phenomenon of the hero's initiation process (*rite de passage*) as the crucial element of maturation, of his 'coming of age'. To insist that the idea of self-realization after an 'identity crisis' is the constitutive element of the twelfth-century romance is admittedly attractive, but it is also to neglect considerable expanses of the texts in question.

More important is the critical spirit with which Chrétien and

his contemporaries treat their themes, themes which are shown
to be problematic and which present the hero with a dilemma
which he has to resolve. It is essentially the chivalry topos, the
coordination of love and chivalry, which acts as the focal point
in which problems are brought into definition. Whilst their
solution may well issue in an enhanced self-consciousness of the
hero and even a new sense of identity, the constitutive feature of
twelfth-century romance is more convincingly identified in its
casuistical nature. The word *casuistical* is used here in its
technical sense of 'concerned with the moral evaluation of
individual case histories and the circumstances peculiar to
them'. The romances represent a corpus of works written by
literary virtuosi, morally uncommitted, it often seems, to a
philosophy or a thesis, but keen to show originality in the
manipulation of conventions. They are the product of a
community of poets engaged in a game of variations, ringing the
changes on a common stock of themes in varying combinations,
often with sly allusions to each other's work. Each romance
deals with one or more *casus*, particular 'cases' or sets of
circumstances, and debates them in the light of familiar propositions and principles, thus constituting a critical investigation
(see Hunt, *52*, Schnell, *76* and Shirt, *78*). It is important to
remind ourselves in this connexion that the study of twelfth-
century romance has suffered from being largely limited to the
works of Chrétien, who, because of his manifest excellence, has
in turn been studied in something of a vacuum, abstracted from
the works of his contemporaries. The latter have consequently
achieved the status of Mark Twain's 'classic': 'something that
everybody wants to have read and nobody wants to read'. This
situation must be remedied if we are not to falsify the picture of
romance writing in Chrétien's time. The following list of works,
with their approximate dates, will serve as a brief reminder of
the context in which the *Yvain* should be studied: *Roman de
Thèbes* (c. 1150+), *Roman d'Eneas* (c. 1155-60), *Roman de
Troie* (c. 1160), *Floire et Blancheflor* (1150-60), Béroul's
Tristran (c. 1160), Gautier d'Arras's *Eracle* (c. 1178-81?) and
Ille et Galeron (1181-83?), Thomas's *Tristan* (c. 1175), Hue de
Rotelande's *Ipomedon* (c. 1180) and *Prothesilaus* (1185-90),

Partonopeus de Blois (1182-85), *Athis et Prophilias* (1180s),
Aimon de Varennes's *Florimont* (dated internally to 1188),
Jaufre (Provençal, in existence in some form before 1200),
Renaud de Bâgé's *Le Bel Inconnu* (before 1200). This collection
of texts represents over four times the total of lines in Chrétien's
œuvre!

A few examples of the 'casuistry' of the romances named
above will illustrate our foregoing contentions. As instances of
the amatory *casus* we have *l'homme entre deux femmes* (Ille
caught between Galeron and Ganor in *Ille et Galeron*), *la femme
entre deux hommes* (Cardïones caught between Athis and
Prophilias in *Athis et Prophilias*, Athanaïs between the Emperor
and Paridés in *Eracle*, Fenice between Alis and Cligés in *Cligés*).
The dialectical debate is a favourite *mise au point* of the *casus*.
Romadanaple in *Florimont* is caught between *Amor* and
Sapience, Gaïte in *Athis et Prophilias* struggles with *Amors* and
Sans, Ille in *Ille et Galeron* with *Amors* and *Pité* (in respect of
Galeron and Ganor). Such moral dilemmas argued out
dialectically are the stuff of much romance writing in the twelfth
century, *Cligés* offering simply the most arduous examples.

Aside from dialectically formulated situations there is a
constant stock of issues examined anew in varying situations and
the subject of conscious attempts at originality by the poets. For
example, what qualities most fittingly inspire love — wealth,
lineage, beauty, chivalric deeds or social class? What is the true
nature of women — are they naturally good, the elect of God's
creatures, or else evil, or changeable or weak or proud? Every
romance writer at some point takes up a position regarding the
long tradition of antifeminism. Is love a discriminating force? If
it is not, what may render it so? How is love instilled in the lover
— through the eyes, the ears, the hands, the breath or the heart?
By what criteria is true love best distinguished from false love
and what is the most adequate terminology? How reliable are
the textbook symptoms of love? As the author of *Florimont*
remarks, all who are pale are not necessarily in love, and, as an
episode in *Cligés* (541ff.) shows, paleness may sometimes be
interpreted as a symptom of sea-sickness. What is the true end of
chivalry — service of a lady (chivalry topos), of fellow knights,

or of the community as a whole? How far should a knight go in subordinating his activities to the wishes of a lady (independently of her character)? Should this lady be his wife? The romances treat these questions, not in the light of conventional morality, but rather in the forum of rival claims and competing opinions.

Then there are intertextual references in the romances which enable us to glimpse the writers' sense of poetic rivalry within a communal enterprise. *Ipomedon* and *Prothesilaus* both contain allusions to or borrowings from the *Tristan* of Thomas. The narrator of *Florimont* takes issue with a passage in *Cligés* on the transmission of love through the eyes, arguing that this is demonstrably misleading since there are those who are loved unseen and that in any case love is often transmitted via the ears and hands. In *Eracle* a passage beginning 'Amors n'a cure de rentier' is a clear allusion to Fenice's rejection of sharing two men in *Cligés* and in another passage Gautier d'Arras takes up the image of the smouldering fire in *Yvain* (ll.1777ff.) as an image of passion and 'corrects' it by dwelling on the strength of the clear flame and reinterpreting the symbolism of the image in an amatory defence of smokeless fuel. In *Prothesilaus* there is a magic fountain which cures toothache and *Jaufre*, which is full of sly allusions to *Yvain*, makes the magic fountain the scene of a fantastic underwater adventure, whilst Jaufre's companions lament his death by drowning. The authors of the courtly romances are well aware of the distance separating their literary games and their audiences' perception of the world around them. Sometimes the romance narrator will even make a comparison or contrast between his own lady and a character in his tale! Uppermost is the notion of game, which embraces the ingenuity of intertextual references, the humorous reslanting of commonplaces, joy in sophistical debate, and a constant undercurrent of self-mocking irony. All these elements can from time to time be discerned in the treatment of one of the romances' most basic themes, *fin' amors* or 'courtly love'. Recently it has come to be recognized that this concept is given both secular and religious dimensions, but critics have not asked themselves whether the multiple meanings of *fin' amors* in the texts are not deliberate, intended for humorous effect, part of the sophisticated rivalry of courtly poets. A survey of Chrétien's contemporaries shows that the term *fin' amors* may be applied to almost every kind of love relationship — friendship between men, heterosexual passion, whether adulterous or not, love of God and so on. Of course, it always denotes loyal, reliable love, but the interest lies in defining loyalty in the varied situations of conflict and choice which the poets deliberately 'set up'.

We thus conclude that in the twelfth century the courtly romance was a critical and playful investigation of 'cases' (*casus*) involving the relationship of love and chivalry, which uses the *merveilleux* both to generate and characterize *aventure* in a way which illustrates the dual tendency of romance, noted by Frye, 'to displace myth in a human direction and yet, in contrast to 'realism', to conventionalize content in an idealized direction' (see *37*, pp.136-37). One of the most intriguing aspects of the romances is the tension created by the coexistence of an idealistic and a critical spirit, the latter frequently undercutting the former, the exact balance of the two varying from work to work. It is this tension which unambiguously marks off the romance from the saint's life which may share some of the characteristic and distinctive features of the romance.

Above all, the romance stands in clear opposition to the epic. Formally the epic or *chanson de geste* proceeds in a paratactic manner, that is, it juxtaposes motifs, scenes and so forth without connectives, forming a string of stanzas (*laisses*) of variable length which exploit the technique of repetition with variation, rather like the phraseology of the liturgy. The latter is also evoked by the frequent use of formulaic half-lines (hemistichs) which are part of the reciter's vast memorized repertoire of improvisatory materials. The use of assonance (agreement of final tonic vowel only), the relatively stable division of the line into 4 + 6 syllables, and the appearance of stanzas repeating the same essential material (*laisses similaires*), lend to the epic a repetitive quality of an almost liturgical nature. In contrast, the romance has a syntactic structure and a progressive movement which is aided by the light rhythm of eight-syllable lines, arranged in couplets, exploiting *enjambement* and grammatical

subordination (*hypotaxis*). The use of set expressions or
formulae is replaced by a striving for lexical variation (see *80*)
and there is a greater variety in tense usage. The epic has a
monumental, sculptured quality characteristic of romanesque
art, whilst the romance exhibits more of the features of Gothic
stained glass: bright, restless, vertical movement. The romance
is syntactic, in that it attends to the relations between things,
whereas the epic juxtaposes elements without explicit indication
of temporal sequence or relation (another parallel with the
liturgy). The romance deals with the solitary quest, rather than
the collective or public expedition favoured by the epic. The epic
is concerned with a world of known values, of duty recognized
in a public arena, and is a celebration or affirmation of these
values. In contrast, the romance is an investigation, an enquiry
after criteria of action by an individual separated from the
collectivity (court). In the epic (and saint's life) the *merveilleux* is
a corroborative phenomenon, a confirmation of the divine will;
in the romance it represents an 'other', as yet unknown, world in
which the hero achieves insights formerly denied him and may
even experience a private epiphany which reorientates his
actions. The epic exploit is replaced by *aventure*. The logical
play of oppositions, which constituted dialectic as a formal
discipline in the twelfth century, is reflected in quite different
ways in the three characteristic genres of the period. In the epic
the opposition of values is resolved by the elimination of one of
the terms of the opposition (e.g. Christians defeat pagans); in
the troubadour lyric such tensions are left unresolved in striking
paradoxes which are the substance of the poet's song; in the
romance they are finally transcended, hence the idealism
associated with this type of literature. It remains, therefore, to
see what the significant oppositions in *Yvain* are and how they
are dealt with.

2. Subversion

'There is Truth in Falsehood,
Falsehood in Truth'
(Browning, A Soul's
Tragedy)

In view of the spirit of dialectic which pervades twelfth-century romance we should not be surprised to find that almost from the beginning the poets are capable of undermining the very values which their works purport to mediate and that a thread of irony runs through the whole development of romance (see Green, *39*). What are perceived, on account of their appropriateness and familiarity, as romance conventions may be displaced by shifting contextual detail so as to appear in constantly changing perspectives which rob them of any definitive or absolute value and leave them to function as either beacons or decoys. Such effects are promoted with sophisticated aplomb quite remote from the rather heavy-handed humour which marks Chaucer's burlesque of the romance and the would-be romance narrator in *The Knight's Tale*. Calogrenant's unsuitability as a courtly narrator, for example, is presented with a subtlety which has eluded many commentators. The initial *mise en scène* of Chrétien's *Yvain* is simply the first of a number of episodes which bring together the three constitutive components of the romance — *amor*, *chevalerie*, and *clergie* — only to reveal their fundamental ambiguity as models or interpretative markers.

At the outset, for example, the theme of love is presented as the true apanage of a distant Arthurian past in which lovers were courtly, brave, generous and honourable. In the present age 'est amors mout abeissiee' (l.20), travestied by those who make only a pretence of loving, divorced from sincerity of feeling. What are we to make of this complaint? Is it merely the rehearsal of a rhetorical commonplace, praise of the past as a Golden Age (*laudatio temporis acti*), at the expense of the contemporary

world? Or are we already being invited to participate in the
search for criteria of judgement by reflecting on the possible
identity of those who 'dient qu'il aimment, mes il mantent'
(l.26)? Or are we being mischievously misled by Chrétien
through his encouragement of false expectations concerning the
story which follows? The latter possibility is certainly suggested
by our later realization that the amatory figures depicted in
Yvain scarcely seem exemplary and by the reflection that there
has never been a greater curiosity about the nature and ramifications of human love than that displayed by Chrétien's contemporaries: it was they who recreated an 'Age of Ovid' (*aetas
Ovidiana*), alert as never before to the subtleties of this master
ironist; it was they who provoked numerous commentaries on
the *Song of Songs*, and who formed appreciative audiences for
the courtly love lyric. Is all this to be dismissed as 'fable et
mançonge' (l.27)? Conversely, the erotic connotations of
Arthur's retreat to the conjugal bedchamber (note especially the
expression *s'oblier*, see Pelan, *69*) do nothing to mitigate what is
clearly depicted as a striking breach of etiquette (see ll.649-52).
Calogrenant's ineffectual dalliance with the daughter of his
hospitable host, Yvain's passion for the woman he has recklessly
widowed, Gawain's absences when ladies are in trouble — these
do not inspire belief in the superiority of Arthur's court in
matters of love (cf. ll.13, 20, 24). It is impossible to overlook the
fact that the opening references to *amors* are never qualified in
such a way as to dispel the basic ambiguity of the term. It could
easily be argued that it is not *eros*, but *amicitia*, friendship,
which actually sustains the most successful relationships of the
romance, namely between Yvain and Lunete, Yvain and the
lion, and Yvain and Gawain. Erotic love, as suggested by the
figures of the Dame de Noroison, the host's daughter at Pesme
Avanture, and by Laudine herself, conspicuously lacks positive
or constructive features. Thus Chrétien's ironical manipulation
of the Golden Age topos applied to love leaves undetermined
both the nature of that love and the conduct of its practitioners.
We are already, therefore, on a semantic quest. By evoking and
then undercutting nostalgia for an idealized past, the narrator
enjoins discrimination on his audience.

The initial presentation of chivalry inspires no greater confidence. The idea that Arthur's renown brings to mind the flower of chivalry and unceasing striving after honour (ll.39-41) is promptly undermined by the adversative *mes* ('but') of line 41 and the descent into bathos with the court's reaction of shock (the adverbial intensifier *mout* is used three times in five lines) at the king's unprecedented abandonment of the pentecostal celebrations, traditionally the greatest festival of the Arthurian calendar. The overturning of expectations ('s'esmerveillierent', l.42) is already inscribed as a theme within the romance, as well as constituting a narrative device directed at the audience. It is marked throughout the introduction by the repeated use of *mes* (ll.18, 26, 29, 42, 49, see Grimbert, *41*). The chivalric image evoked by the introduction of Arthur's knights is also inverted by the unexpected discovery that Calogrenant is relating 'un conte, / non de s'enor, mes de sa honte' (ll.59-60) and by the uncourtly squabbling which is precipitated by the arrival of the queen. This heralds another surprise, since a celebrated convention of the Arthurian tradition was that Arthur would not eat until he had news of an adventure (see, for example, Chrétien's *Conte du graal*, ll.2822ff.). Here, though, he eats *first* and it is his *wife* who is anxious for 'noveles', indeed surprisingly insistent that Calogrenant tell his story, despite his obvious reluctance and the fact that the disagreeable Kay, who is *ex professo* malicious, is demanding the same thing.

In common with Chrétien's actual audience, therefore, the fictional audience within the romance receives a number of surprises. We may already begin to wonder whether the epithets *buens*, *preu* and *cortois*, associated with Arthur in the opening lines of the romance, are merely ornamental rather than operational. They seem incongruous with his actions so far and later (ll.1004-15) Lunete will complain of the discourtesy which she experienced on an earlier visit to the court, when only Yvain deigned to speak to her. Is there an intended irony in the expression 'la cui proesce nos ansaingne' (l.1), a hint that Arthur does not always exemplify the virtues which he holds up to others? Certainly, the exemplar of Arthurian chivalry, Gawain, later gives the hero advice which he freely admits he would be unlikely to follow himself (ll.2533-38). Chrétien's systematic undercutting of conventional expectations generates in the audience a discomfort and insecurity which can only be attenuated by a critical response to the scenes which unfold before its uncertain gaze.

This problem of reception is itself represented in the romance by Calogrenant's formal attempt to gain the goodwill of his audience (*captatio benevolentiae*) (ll.149-74) in which we are invited to 'gloss' his tale aright. The tale, too, contains a number of reversals: the meeting with the beautiful maiden is inconclusive and the hospitable host, an entirely conventional figure, cannot recall when he last entertained a 'chevalier errant, / qui avanture alast querant' (ll.259-60), in spite of the fact that it is his traditional role to do precisely this! His request that Calogrenant repay his hospitality by according him another visit on his return journey and the latter's somewhat condescending response are both ironic in the light of future events. The confrontation of knight and herdsman produces a striking inversion of roles. The knight errant is fearful and uncomprehending (he suspects the herdsman is a shape-shifting, supernatural creature, rather than a man), his chivalry purposeless and ineffectual. The *vilain*, on the other hand, is quietly confident, mild-mannered, assured of his humanity ('Je sui uns hon', l.330), and executes his functions as a herdsman with demonstrable efficiency and success. As a human he can appreciate the existence of a *mervoille* (the fountain), but there is no room in his practically ordered life for *avanture*, a concept entirely lacking in significance for him. Yet, the herdsman's description of the fountain phenomenon and its dangers (ll.404-07) alone explains the host's special interest in Calogrenant's return and also the absence of recent visitors, though it is doubtful if Calogrenant himself perceives the connection. The naively curious knight is quickly disillusioned, however, and is soon fighting for his life. He is himself prompt to anticipate defeat and allows the fountain knight to make off with his horse. He retreats to the fountain to recover, the loss of his mount and the imprudent dumping of his arms symbolizing his forfeiture of chivalric status. Yet he lives to tell the tale, much to the surprise of the hospitable host and his daughter! Arthurian chivalry appears to be a bewildering phenomenon and the values which subtend it anything but clear.

So far, then, the audience receives a most unpromising impression of *amor* and *chevalerie* — against all expectations! And so we come to the third basic component of courtly romance, *clergie*. The learning of the author is perhaps already apparent in the introductory use of the 'indirect approach' (*insinuatio*) (see Hunt, *49*, pp.5, 11ff.), probable etymological play on 'tant coste' and '*pan*tecoste' (ll.5-6), in the ironic inversion of *Ecclesiastes* IX,4 ('A living dog is better than a dead lion') in the *sententia* 'Qu'ancor vaut miauz, ce m'est vis, / uns cortois morz qu'uns vilains vis' (ll.31-32), and in the allusion to the Breton myth of Arthur's return (ll.37-38), which is ironically attenuated to 'toz jorz mes vivra ses nons'. But the real subversion of courtly *clergie* is to be found in the burlesquing of the courtly narrator and his pretensions in Calogrenant's 'prologue' (*exordium*) and narrative (*narratio*), an account whose length stands in comic contrast to the brevity of the chivalric combat which is its culmination. This extremely reluctant narrator, provided with a captive audience by the queen's command, prefaces his tale — quite unnecessarily, it would seem — with a *captatio benevolentiae* which is indistinguishable in content and style from the literary prologues of the courtly romancers themselves. Not only is the distinction of *oïr* — *antandre*, *oroilles* — *cuer*, a literary topos, but the idea and phraseology of lines 171-73 are entirely in the style of Chrétien himself (cf. ll.24, 27 and the prologue of *Erec*). For all the familiarity of this motif of 'right understanding', it is anything but clear how it is to be applied to the tale which Calogrenant relates, which is told with the same naivety that the provincial Julien Sorel displays in reporting his riding mishap at the Hôtel de la Mole. It is true that Calogrenant's performance is far from artless and is obviously justificatory in tone, but what gloss can be put on it save discreet acknowledgement of the knight's *folie* and respect for his honesty?

As in the case of reversal of expectations, an aspect of Chrétien's relationship with his audience is here inscribed as a theme in the romance, namely the notion of narrative performance and interpretation — the problem in short, of reception. Calogrenant's story is begun, in fact, no fewer than four times: by Calogrenant to his assembled companions, by Calogrenant to the queen, by the queen to Arthur, and finally, in modified form, by Yvain to Arthur on the latter's arrival at the fountain (ll.2291ff.). It is possible to argue that Calogrenant self-consciously appropriates the exordial rhetoric of courtly narrative to conceal the dismal failure of his enterprise and to bolster the belief that the story is not so superficial or negative as it seems — if we take Calogrenant as speaking in his own voice. But Chrétien's unique abrogation of a formal prologue in the *Yvain* may lead us to suspect that it is the voice of Chrétien Narrator speaking to us (cf. Grigsby, *40*) and alerting us to the task of interpretation, not merely of Calogrenant's adventure, but of the whole romance. If, as we have suggested, interpretation is explicitly incorporated into the thematic texture of the romance, we should not be surprised by such an act of transference by which narratorial argument is presented through a fictional character. But then the play of differing viewpoints makes possible the ironizing of interpretation itself. Perhaps we are invited to evaluate Calogrenant's own interpretation of his experience and its reception by his listeners. The irony would arise from the contrast of his narrative ambitions with his poor chivalric performance, Calogrenant's attempt to imply exegetical complexities in his narrative appearing far-fetched, part of a burlesque of narrative interpretation. Irony might also be located in the fact that nobody at court does appear to interpret his story correctly, since the problem produced by the unannounced hostilities against the fountain knight (he complains about the lack of a *défi*, ll.491ff.) goes entirely unnoticed by Calogrenant's audience.

Let us look more closely at the courtly rhetoric of Calogrenant's narrative. He begins with the unexpected revelation that his adventure took place (*avint*) seven years previously. Literal acceptance of this indication would be surprising, for there is no apparent motive for its present disclosure after so long an interval (his return to court unarmed and on foot would surely have frustrated concealment) nor any ready explanation of the ardour of the court's response. In fact, the number seven is a conventional figure denoting an indeterminate passage of time (cf. l.2089, Laudine has been married for seven years). Another literary convention is the path to the right ('chemin a destre', l.80) which is normally indicative of success and is here ironically inverted to suggest the gap between Calogrenant's selection of detail and his own limited comprehension of what happened to him. He evokes the image of the knight errant alongside that of the *païsanz* (l.176), forming an oxymoron which neatly anticipates the confrontation of *chevalier* and *vilain* in the forest. The *brevitas* formula (l.252), assurances of veracity (ll.284, 430f., 526f.), and the *sententia* (l.457f.) are common features of courtly narrative. How, then, is this story to be 'de cuer antandue' (l.152)? Calogrenant's own interpretation never goes beyond seeing it as *folie* (ll.434f., 477, 551f., 577ff.). His comments are frequently naive (ll.337ff., 416ff., 439ff., 451ff.). Above all, there are two crucial features of his account which give pause for reflexion. First, this nervous, irresolute knight has little understanding of knight errantry, offering to the herdsman a definition so vacuous as to undermine the traditional superiority of the knights (*milites*) to the peasants (*rustici*). Second, whilst reporting in significant detail the complaint made against him by the fountain knight (ll.491-516), Calogrenant shows no recognition of its force or validity, despite his own assertion that 'parole oïe est perdue / s'ele n'est de cuer antandue' (ll.151-52). Does the court understand any better? Certainly, Yvain never shows the slightest acknowledgement that the fountain knight has been wronged and he straightway conceives a mission of vengeance. Arthur's reaction is modulated differently. He hears the story at second hand from the queen, another courtly narrator 'que bien et bel conter li sot' (l.660), and his promise to take the court to 'see' (l.665) the fountain evokes the notion of a tourist excursion rather than revenge. It is true that Laudine receives advance warning of the expedition from the Dameisele Sauvage (ll.1619ff.), but it is hopelessly unclear whether this figure is a spokesman of Arthur's court or a *confidente*/scout of Laudine. The question remains, therefore, whether anybody recognizes the gravamen of the fountain knight's complaint and thus discerns the implications of Calogrenant's tale for the maintenance of feudal justice. A general *ignoratio elenchi* or failure to grasp the point at issue leaves the legal question of the unprovoked devastation of the lands around the fountain unanswered, the hero simply repeating the offence first complained of. Calogrenant's narrative performance thus embodies the fundamental problem of courtly interpretation and reception. His narrative pretensions, his *clergie*, are placed in ironic contrast with his naive incomprehension of the chivalric *métier*, whilst at the same time they are apparently unsuccessful in procuring the 'right understanding' of his audience. Chrétien himself must hope for something better!

Thus, in his *mise en scène* Chrétien has already subverted the essential romance constituents of *amor*, *chevalerie* and *clergie* by depicting failure in all three, thereby overturning audience expectations. The coordination of *amor* and *chevalerie* mediated by the *clergie* of an interpreter is again subjected to critical investigation in the episode of Pesme Avanture, significantly the greatest challenge which the hero has to meet and one which conspicuously involves the problems of appearance and reality. As Yvain and a young maiden, in need of lodging for the night, approach the town of Pesme Avanture, they are met by the vituperations of a hostile crowd who warn them against entering the town. In the lines 'La, ou tu vas, t'an iert tant fet, / que ja par toi n'iert reconté' (ll.5134-35) we may detect a reminiscence of the herdsman's warning to Calogrenant (ll.404-07), but we retain a precarious hope that the hero will 'sanz trop grant honte revenir' (l.5173).

The rhetoric of hostility, however, must be carefully interpreted if it is to be correctly understood, and so a lady 'cortoise et sage' (l.5144) assists Yvain as interpreter by explaining that the unwelcoming greeting is extended to every *prodome*, in order to discourage him from becoming involved in an adventure from which he cannot return. Apparent animosity thus disguises true compassion. Yet, such a strategy, which requires correct understanding, forms a contrast with the spontaneity of the hero's intuitive reaction: '... mes fos [in the Guiot MS, *fins*] cuers leanz me tire, / si ferai ce, que mes cuers viaut' (ll.5176-77). This reaction is clearly different from the hero's former recklessness in the fountain adventure, but a similar uncertainty remains as to whether he acts *en pleine connaissance de cause*. He advances past an abusive porter and comes to a large building behind an enclosure in which three hundred silkworkers, all of them women, toil in poverty. Again Yvain is in need of an explanation and this is duly afforded by one of the workers who explains that their plight is the result of the knight-errantry of a young king, who, like a 'fos naïs' rode out 'por aprendre noveles' (l.5258). The parallel with Calogrenant is obvious. Like Calogrenant, the young king was weaker than his opponent(s) and suffered defeat. A tribute of thirty maidens a year was exacted as the price of his freedom. This account, like Calogrenant's tale, is no *fable* (l.5272) and all too clearly issued in *honte* (ll.5117, 5133, 5173, 5220, 5264, 5267, 5292).

What we have here is the *mise en abyme* (see Dällenbach, *27*) of chivalric adventure, that is to say, the hero's exploit at this point in the romance itself enshrines or mirrors a typically romance adventure. These adventures are mediated by accounts — those of Calogrenant, the silkworker, the host of Pesme Avanture — which themselves require interpretation. This juxta-position of chivalric adventure and narrative is now significantly followed by a purely literary vignette. Just as we sense that we have witnessed a thematic strand of chivalric romance incor-porated within a romance adventure, Chrétien consolidates the typically romance nexus of *amor*, *chevalerie* and *clergie* by intro-ducing the picture of the young girl reading to her parents 'an un romanz, ne sai de cui' (l.5366). The sly affectation of ignorance by the narrator positively invites an ironic interpretation as an allusion to Chrétien. Be that as it may, the scene inevitably emphasizes the fictionality of the romance, whilst the broader context of Pesme Avanture has already stressed the importance of interpretation. The whole episode resonates with ironic echoes and subversive strategies. First of all, there is the provocative contrast between the forced labour of the impoverished silkworkers and the comfortable leisure of the romance reciter and her audience. Does this not point to a

corresponding incongruity between the poetic fictions of
Chrétien's own romances and the harsh realities of medieval
life? — unless, of course, the romances are carefully interpreted!
Second, there is the puzzling discrepancy between the narrator's
courtly preciosity in evoking the love theme and his return to the
disparaging claim, already made in the prologue, that his contemporaries are not interested in love (ll.5374-96). Third,
reading from a romance heralds the highly ironic manipulation
of the chivalry topos, the essential structural feature of the
romance genre, through a number of devices which upset
normal expectations. Having penetrated to the heart of the
castle, Yvain is suddenly no longer the maligned alien, but the
welcome liberator — at least, it looks as if he is, but the narrator
will not relinquish his caution about appearance and reality: 'Je
ne sai, se il le deçoivent, / mes a grant joie le reçoivent / et font
sanblant, que il lor pleise, / que herbergiez soit a grant eise'
(ll.5407-10). The earlier reaction of hostility has been reversed
'Or doint Des, que trop ne li cost / ceste *losange* et cist *servise*'
(ll.5424-25). The reluctant liberator (he wishes to depart after a
single night) is *not* inspired by love of the host's daughter
(ll.5479ff.), yet even before he has defeated his opponents, she is
all but forced upon him (ll.5486ff.). This ironic use of the *don
contraignant* (see Frappier, *34* and Ménard, *63*) recalls Yvain's
earlier exploitation of the device when seeking leave from
Laudine (ll.2549ff.).

In undertaking the adventure Yvain is almost bound to accept
the hand of the host's daughter if he is successful. But the
chivalry topos is here effectively dismantled. We witness, not the
coordination of love and chivalry, but the disjunction of the
two. Yvain's chivalric intervention is made under duress
(ll.5462ff. and esp. 5506-11) and it is also under duress that he
receives the maiden's submission which compels him to lie to his
host and promise to return. The act of liberation, the release of
the captive silkworkers, is an afterthought, substituted for
acceptance of the host's daughter who is almost forced on the
hero (ll.5703ff.). Yvain stands accused of *orguel* (l.5742) and lies
to the host (ll.5750-55)! This is a most peculiar adventure! It is
tempting to render Pesme Avanture by 'Terrible Adventure' to

indicate that it is both fear-inducing and a very bad, that is, untypical, one. The conventional motivation of chivalric adventure and its customary reward are strikingly undermined. To a certain extent (the silkworkers admittedly regain their freedom) Pesme Avanture represents an ironic subversion of romance adventure. That it includes a direct allusion to romance reading confirms our view that in the *Yvain* Chrétien sets out to challenge many of the assumptions of courtly romance.

The conclusion of the work provides further evidence of subversion and the dismantling of the chivalry topos. It provides no indication at all that Yvain's chivalric exploits constitute a *service d'amour*, inspired by love of Laudine. Indeed, it is only after his labours are over that we have unambiguous evidence of his love (ll.6511ff.). It is true that at the incognito meeting with Laudine the latter is described as 'la dame, qui avoit / son cuer' (ll.4583-84), but this is no more than confirmation of what has already been established: that the two exchanged hearts (ll.2639ff.). It certainly does not of itself justify the view that the adventures of the second part of the romance are undertaken in Laudine's service or for the purpose of rehabilitating the hero in her eyes. The despair with which Yvain finally returns to the fountain implies, rather, that he has little confidence that he will be accepted as a reformed character. It is not in merit that he places his hope, but in the coercive power of storm raising at the fountain ('par force et par estovoir', l.6522). If love-service is missing from the reconciliation, so is reward. Not for one moment does Laudine concede that Yvain has deserved forgiveness and not a loving word does she utter. The full extent of the concession which she grants to her knight and husband is: 'I'd rather put up with tempests and storms for the rest of my life and, were it not perjury, which is a wicked and evil thing, I should never grant him reconciliation at any price ... I accept reconciliation, since I should be committing perjury if I did not do everything in my power to secure reconciliation between us' (ll.6766-71, 6790-93). Ovid's 'I shall hate, if I can; if not I shall love against my will' (*Amores* 3,11,35) would seem to offer an accurate summary of the attitude adopted by Laudine, who displays none of the humility which she had shown earlier to

Lunete (ll.1794ff.). Instead of the chivalry topos mediated by courtly *clergie*, we have the potent combination of physical coercion (the storm at the fountain) with fear of perjury induced by a *pia fraus* ('Bien m'avez au hoquerel prise', l.6761), all made possible by the *consoil* and *san* of Lunete 'qui mout fu cortoise' (l.6630), extracting the oath from her mistress 'mout cortoisemant' (l.6635). This is the final irony — that *cortois* should be associated with a dénouement so absolutely at odds with the conventions of courtly romance.

Yvain is, at least in part, an ironic study of courtly romance which examines two problems: the reception of courtly narrative and the relation of love and chivalry. The traditional bride-winning motif is consistently undercut. The hero seeks revenge for a kinsman's shame and finds a wife in the widow of the man he slays. Marriage is achieved through the stage-managing of a wily *entremetteuse* and the dictates of power politics. Arthur is an unwitting catalyst in this process, for his apparently 'friendly' visit is interpreted as a planned invasion of the lady's territories. The hero suddenly finds himself a poacher turned gamekeeper, the beneficiary of a Pyrrhic victory over a craven court and an apparently grief-stricken widow. How seriously can a marriage which rests upon such a basis be taken? When, after a lengthy separation, the partners are reunited by a process almost identical with the one which first brought them together, is not a degree of scepticism amply justified? The narrator's strained gloss on the reconciliation is so at variance with what we have witnessed as to invite doubt by its very incongruity: 'Ore a mes sire Yvains sa pes, / *si poez croire*, qu'onques mes / ne fu de rien nule si liez, / comant qu'il et esté iriez. / Mout an est a buen chief venuz; / qu'il est amez et chier tenuz / de sa dame, et ele de lui' (ll.6799-805). Only by assuming an ironic intention could we find here confirmation of the claim by Chaucer's Pandarus 'the ende is every tales strengthe'. The contrived circularity of plot would then be seen as an illustration of the maxim *finis origine pendet* — the end corresponds with the beginning.

Another theme which radically overturns conventional expectations is the friendship of Yvain and Gawain. Their relationship is first mentioned in Marie de France's *Lai de*

Lanval, but it is not illustrated before the *Yvain*. On the other hand, in Chrétien's earlier romances Gawain is closely associated with the hero (see Busby, *20*). Yet, here there is a significant contrary motion: as Yvain's stock initially falls, Gawain's rises, whilst after the crisis the movement is reversed. Paradoxically, Gawain is first mentioned in the text in conjunction with Kay, his opposite, as part of Calogrenant's audience (l.55) and the second reference to him is also made in connexion with Kay, for the two men, despite their dissimilarity, are twinned in Yvain's imagination as rivals to his claim on priority in avenging Calogrenant's shame (ll.683-90). The paragon of chivalry turns out to be more dangerous to the hero than the personification of slander, who at first achieves ascendancy in Yvain's state of mind during the pursuit of the fountain knight (ll.1348ff.), but is quickly disposed of in their confrontation at the fountain (ll.2228ff.). Gawain, who has defended Yvain's courtesy towards Kay (ll.2212ff.), is overjoyed at his friend's victory, for 'he loved his company more than that of any other knight he knew' (ll.2288-90). Yet, soon afterwards, and following the narrator's encomium of him as he who illuminates chivalry as the sun irradiates the morning (ll.2400ff.), Gawain appears before Yvain and presses him to take leave of his wife and accompany him to the tournaments. Nothing in his speech (ll.2484-538) can be taken as a really serious appraisal of Yvain's interests (he admits that in his friend's position he would not observe his own instructions, l.2527ff.). Rather, he takes over the role already adopted by the Arthurian company which has campaigned the whole week long in an unsuccessful effort to get Yvain, just married, to depart with them (ll.2479-83). Gawain acts on the same impulse which has already led him to befriend Lunete: sheer joy at finding that his friend's life has been saved.

It is quite wrong, therefore, to see in Gawain's arguments before Yvain a programmatic statement which receives public endorsement. It is a farrago of courtly themes, half digested, designed to produce a sense of unease in a newly wed *ex ephebis* — from the ranks of youth. Gawain's friendly advice is inimical to the hero. Here we have the subversion of the traditional motif of *compagnonnage*, for not only does Gawain secure his friend's imprudent departure, but it is also he who directly causes Yvain to outstay his leave (ll.2674ff.). This unconventional handling of the theme of *amicitia* is extended in a series of further paradoxes. The chivalry topos is inverted: knightly deeds lead the hero *away from* the lady! Gawain's unavailability on a number of occasions when he is sorely needed by relatives, whilst rendering his chivalry somewhat problematic (when he is free to intervene, he backs what is manifestly the wrong side), actually permits Yvain to act as a surrogate and thereby to ascend in knightly worth. As Yvain's stature increases, Gawain's seems to diminish. The conjunction of friendship and enmity in the two friends receives an ingenious rhetorical elaboration at the moment of their incognito combat (ll.6001ff.) which may be designed to suggest the same paradox of the relationship of Yvain and Laudine and, by the same token, to prepare their reconciliation. There is never the slightest explicit criticism of Gawain. He is never blamed for Yvain's overstaying of his leave or for supporting the unjust side in the inheritance dispute. Yvain shows no resentment, his affection for Gawain remaining undiminished (ll.6284-91). Despite all this, Gawain fails to coordinate love and chivalry and is responsible for the disjunction of the two in the hero. He is thus crucially associated with the subversion of the chivalry topos in the romance, possessing, like Arthur, courtly status, but not moral authority.

3. Malitia — militia

In the twelfth century the legitimacy of warfare was incontestable (whereas that of pacifism was not), but the spirit and manner in which it might be conducted were keenly and anxiously debated (see Contamine, *24*). Military activity without the informing principle of justice was seen to be uncoordinated violence in the service of self interest, a brutal adventurism perpetrated by little more than thugs who called themselves knights. The profit motive reigned supreme (Cicero called money 'the sinews of war'). Chivalry was less an ideal than a problem. Throughout the eleventh and twelfth centuries a long line of churchmen identified in secular knighthood a shameless indulgence in rapine, homicide, and wasteful ostentation. According to the report of Fulcher of Chartres (c.1100-06) Urban II preached the First Crusade at the Council of Clermont in 1095 with the words 'Now let those become soldiers, who were formerly plunderers. Let those rightfully ride out against the pagans, who previously fought against their own brothers and kinsmen. Let them now obtain eternal reward, who before became mercenaries for small cash'.

The attempt to convert chivalric ambitions from material profit to spiritual salvation was continued by St Bernard in his *De laude novae militiae*, written soon after 1130 for the Templars under their master Hugh of Payns. Here he listed as common motives of fighting the impulse of thoughtless anger, the appetite for vainglory, and cupidity for worldly possessions. The 'new' soldiers will bear armaments, not ornaments, their minds will be on the fight, not on display, on victory, not glory, they will inspire fear, not admiration, and will substitute prudence, self-control and cool deliberation for violence, impetuosity and recklessness. The result, says Bernard, will be *militia* (soldiering) instead of *malitia* (malice) — the word-play becomes a leitmotiv throughout the rest of the century, hence the title of our chapter. After Bernard on the 'Soldier of Christ' (*miles Christi*, see Harnack, *46*), an important analysis of the condition and duties of knights is made by John of Salisbury in Book VI of his influential *Policraticus* (1159), a vast treatise on the government of the commonwealth based on an almost unprecedented familiarity with the entire Justinianean corpus of Roman law. The opposition *militia — malitia* constantly reappears. The knight is bound by election and oath to serve justice (*aequitas*) and the common weal (*publica utilitas*), to protect the Church, combat evil, respect the clergy, defend the poor, keep the peace, and to shed his own blood (even lay down his life, if need be) for the good of his fellows. The privileges accorded to knights enjoin on them discipline and loyalty. They must abjure greed, vainglory, intemperance and selfishness. Some fifty years earlier Honorius of Autun had written in his *Elucidarium*, cast as a dialogue, in three books, between master and pupil and designed for the instruction of the clergy, 'What do you think of knights?' To the pupil's question the master replies 'Not much' and lists the commonest vices: knights live off booty and plunder, expropriate lands, and extort ransoms. This picture of selfish brutality was evidently felt to be insufficiently comprehensive and was elaborated in many manuscripts to include the plundering of churches, oppression of widows and orphans, imprisonment of the innocent, pride and envy, falsehood and perjury.

The picture can be endlessly replicated. There are constant reminders of Augustine's caution: *militare* means to serve, but it is sinful to do so for gain (*praeda*) or for the promotion of one's own interests (*rem familiarem*). We recall that since St Paul and the Rule of St Benedict knighthood has been a metaphor of spiritual combat — Alan of Lille at the end of the twelfth century calls it a *figura* and explains that without a proper orientation *exterior militia* is simply 'vain and empty' (*inanis et vacua*). Contemporary knights, complains Alan in his treatise on preaching (*Summa de arte praedicatoria*), prostitute knighthood by their pursuit of gain, becoming aggressors rather than defenders, robbers rather than soldiers. Peter of Blois in the same period paints a garish picture of overblown chivalry, sunk in depravity and addicted to every kind of indulgence and material show, effeminate, gluttonous and feckless. It is easy to recognize the exaggerations of prurient clerics, but it is nonetheless noteworthy that there is no acknowledgement of a secular ethos of chivalry which we have learned to extract from the romances. The activities of knights had become a social problem (see Hunt, *54*).

Yet, warfare was not something that the Church could afford to prohibit. It had, instead, to be controlled. Since Augustine, whose views constantly underwent modification, but for whom war was never anything other than a regrettable necessity, the Church had sought to come to terms with the notion of the just war by a process of development and refinement (see Russell, *74*). It was considered in two aspects: the question of the right to make war (*jus ad bellum*) and the problem of what was acceptable in the conduct of war (*jus in bello*). The first was answered on the basis of theological arguments and canonical texts, producing the three desiderata elaborated later by Aquinas: proper authority, just cause, rightful intent. The response to the second problem was determined largely by civil law, by the *jus gentium* (the moral conventions held to be common to men of all nations) and by feudal ideology, that is, by secular arguments. Since Adalbero of Laon's celebrated division of the 'three orders' of feudal society (churchmen, knights and peasants) in the third decade of the eleventh century, knights had been associated with the protection of the Church, widows and orphans. But if these were their friends, who then were their enemies?

In the eleventh century, in movements known as the Peace and the Truce of God, the Church sought to establish immunity from attack for non-combatants (defined mostly by their social function and inability to bear arms, the *imbelle* or *inerme vulgus*) and to restrict the times of the year and the week when war might be waged among Christians — with what success one can imagine (see Cowdrey, *26*). In addition the Second Lateran Council of 1139 placed a prohibition on the use of certain weapons among Christians, singling out the crossbow (and bow and arrow generally) which was distasteful to Church and nobility alike. By the middle of the century, shortly before the emergence of the chivalric romance in France, the debate on war is given prominence by the appearance (c.1148) of Gratian's *Decretum*, a massive compendium of canon law texts, systematically organized for the first time (along dialectical lines). Inescapably, therefore, and most importantly, the chivalric exploits of the romance hero take their place in a continuum of lay and ecclesiastical concern about warfare. The heroes of *Beowulf*, the *Battle of Maldon* and the *Chanson de Roland* had not been unqualified successes. The Cistercian influence which created the spiritual purity of a Galahad was not to be felt till the beginning of the next century. The chivalric romances of the twelfth century had an interesting transitional role to play.

The introduction of the *Yvain* begins with an evocation of the flower of Arthurian chivalry from which we perforce prescind as we attend to Calogrenant's tale of shame. Calogrenant is naive, but not delinquent. His understanding of knight-errantry ('avantures por esprover / ma proesce et mon hardemant', ll.362f.) is inadequate, hence his lack of success — 'Je sui ... uns chevaliers, / qui quier ce, que trover ne puis' (ll.358-59). He is *aberrant*, since his chivalry is informed by no constructive purpose, whereas within the limitations of his different *ordo* the herdsman is able, despite his static existence, to demonstrate his functional efficiency. *Avanture* means nothing to him, since it is vacuous in Calogrenant's definition, but he is, of course, able to recognize the marvellous or extraordinary. In his description of the *mervoille* of the fountain the herdsman makes no reference to a knightly defender, as if combat with an unknown opponent were too gratuitous to merit acknowledgement. The fountain knight himself, on the other hand, provides an explicit verbal gloss on the encounter.

In a folktale type of narrative this verbal reaction would be quite out of place, for it is the function of the unknown knight to defend the fountain and to be summoned by the storm, but the romance may be used for broader critical purposes. Esclados's (he is not named till l.1970) complaint against his aggressor is twofold: his lands have been devastated by an act of war, and this was initiated without any prior declaration of hostilities (ll.491-516). The absence of a formal challenge (*desfi*, *desfiance*, *desfiement*) is indisputably a significant omission. Whatever attempts were made in the twelfth century to restrict private warfare and the feud (*faida*) and however unsuccessful judicial control might be, there was never any dispute that undeclared attack amounted to *traïson*, a breaking of faith (the aggressor is called a *violator fidei*) and merited rigorous punishment. Some documents mention a period of forty days' notice (cf. *Yvain* ll.3691, 4803), whilst a minimum of three days' advance warning seems to have been generally accepted. Significantly, Gratian in his discussion of the just war introduced a quotation from Isidore which rendered a formal declaration indispensable. Admittedly, Isidore's phraseology was sometimes tampered with, but a formal announcement of hostilities was the rule (cf. *Chanson de Roland* ll.2000ff., *Conte du graal* ll.4759ff.). There are clear traces of legal terminology in Esclados's remonstration (e.g. *triues ne pes*, l.516) which encourage us to see the romance within the ethical framework provided by contemporary law. Those who doubt the latter's relevance on the grounds that it reflects an ideal rather than current practice need to ponder the manifestly idealistic depiction of the hero's conduct (in a number of legal situations!) in the later part of *Yvain*. It is clear that the chivalric ethos of the romances had some influence on the thirteenth-century vogue for allegorical treatises on the virtues and duties of the ideal knight (see, for example, Raoul de Houdenc's *Roman des ailes*).

Now, whilst it is certain that the fountain knight's complaint is a legitimate one, it must follow from the narrative situation that it is the offence and not the offender which stands to be condemned, for Calogrenant was completely ignorant of the aggressive and destructive effect of raising the storm (the herdsman presents it as an individual test of endurance, with no mention of an opponent or of the devastation of lands). There is no question of the moral imputability of his action, however misguided or unfortunate it was. The hero's response to Calogrenant's defeat, however, is more problematic than the critics have allowed. If we were to distrust, with Nietzsche, 'all those in whom the impulse to punish is powerful', we should, of course, be guilty of a great anachronism. Nevertheless, though war might find a just origin in the avenging of injuries, it had to be declared by a constituted authority and not waged unilaterally by an individual, for private war was *eo ipso* unjust. Yvain's impatient resolution, when he already knows of the fountain knight's complaint, is objectionable. He knows, too, that the 'constituted authority' is King Arthur, by whose boon or gift adventures are accorded to the knights at court. Although Arthur does not actually promise to avenge Calogrenant (note the use of *veoir* at ll.665 and 2218), Yvain certainly assumes that he will, suffering anguish at the thought that Kay and Gawain will be given first option on combat with the enemy. The complete isolation of the hero here (*seus* is repeated at ll.679, 693, and 725) is ominous.

In contrast to the joy and gladness which possess every other member of the court, Yvain is depicted as morose and preoccupied — precisely because he wished to go to the fountain alone and the king has now sworn to mount his own expedition (whether as tourist or avenger is a little unclear). Quite simply, Yvain is not satisfied with taking third place after Kay and Gawain: 'Mes il ne les atandra mie, / qu'il n'a soing de lor conpaignie, / einçois ira toz seus son vuel / ou a sa joie ou a son duel' (ll.691-94). Later in the romance he will fight with both of them! At this point Yvain's single-minded determination to preempt them, arrogating to himself a right which belongs properly to his monarch, coupled with the oath of secrecy he imposes on his squire (see ll.739-43), reveals how far the honour of the court is from his mind. His clandestine departure and uncompromising neglect of constituted authority can only place in doubt his *bona fides*. With the combat at the fountain doubts multiply, but Yvain's wilfulness has already been subjected to ironic commentary in the sarcastic response of Kay, whose words bring into relief the hero's departure from protocol and social rectitude: 'Do tell us when you are embarking on this grisly adventure ... and whatever happens, I beseech you, don't depart without taking your leave of us' (ll.604-09). There is particular irony in the promise of legal officers (*prevost, voiier,* l.606) as escort, as if Kay regarded Yvain's decision as unjustified or illegal. The hero's protestations that he is above being provoked include the aphorism that quarrels are not started by those who deal the first blow but by those who retaliate ('se revange', l.643), an ironic reflection of his own mission of vengeance (ll.747-49), a mission which commences as the avenging of Calogrenant's shame, but develops into an attempt to avenge himself on Kay for these very taunts! And, of course, in turn Esclados's own barons will seek to avenge *him* (l.1058)!

An incipient egocentricity in Yvain is rapidly reinforced by the combat with the fountain knight. Again, despite his fore-knowledge, no challenge is issued and the two knights fight without a word being exchanged. At first chivalric decorum is observed: neither combatant seeks to injure the other's horse and thereby secure combat on foot. The narrator comments favourably on this honourable course (ll.855ff.), as if to prepare the contrast with what follows. Yvain deals his opponent such a blow that his mail is stained with blood and brain. That the wound is very obviously a mortal one is explained not only by the fountain knight's flight, but also by the narrator's comment that he was right to flee ('n'ot mie tort', l.873). This is not cowardice therefore. Just when we recall the words of Turnus to Aeneas (*Aen*. 12, 938) 'Let not your enmity go any further', we are presented with Yvain's ruthless pursuit of the dying man. This is problematic on more than one count.

Yvain's treatment of Esclados forms an evident contrast to the latter's dealing with Calogrenant, who was left alone after being knocked from his horse and suffered no further injury (it is difficult to tell from ll.542f. how far Calogrenant felt dis-honoured by his opponent's disdain — the fountain knight does take his horse, just as Yvain himself takes Kay's horse after defeating him at the fountain, ll.2258ff.). The vengeance dis-played now is excessive and disproportionate to the offence. It is quite in contradiction of canon law which admitted revenge (*ultio*) on condition that it did not involve unrestrained violence or needless cruelty: mercy was always to be shown to the defeated (we shall see later that this property is connected with Yvain's lion). Gratian's *Decretum* collects quite unambiguous authorities on this question. Not only does Yvain's pursuit of

Esclados contrast with the treatment of Calogrenant and the prescriptions of canon law, it also contrasts with the hero's later treatment of Count Alier in an episode which has inescapable parallels with the present situation. Then Yvain pursues Alier to one of his castles where his surrender is accepted and pledges taken that peace and restitution will be made (ll.3274ff.). The pacific conclusion of the adventure is entirely consonant with the ordinances of the Church. Thus Yvain's pursuit of the mortally wounded Esclados seems illegitimate by reference to both external and internal evidence.

A more explicit indication of the moral status of his action is conveyed by the narrator's examination of his motives. The narrator has already shown himself to be sensitive to the niceties of chivalric etiquette (ll.855ff.) and has protected Esclados from the imputation of cowardice (l.873). What is unexpected is the fierceness and impetuosity of Yvain's pursuit — a gerfalcon pursuing the crane (such nature imagery reinforces the impression of violence). As if Caligula's 'strike him so that he feels death upon him' were ringing in his ears, Yvain grabs at his opponent from behind, clearly hearing his groans of agony. This ferocious zeal has one cause — not the avenging of a kinsman, the ostensible motive (ll.589, 748f.), which is already definitively achieved by the withdrawal of Esclados, but fear of Kay's taunts and the need to counter them with visible tokens (ll.892ff.). Although Yvain had declared himself indifferent to these taunts (*ranposnes*, ll.630ff.), they cause him bitter anguish during his imprisonment in the fountain knight's castle (ll.1348ff., threefold repetition of *ranposnes*). It is a significant irony that Yvain's overwhelming need of *ansaignes veraies* (l.899) or *tesmoing* (ll.1344, 1346, cf. 1533-35) to convince Kay arises entirely from his self-imposed condition of undertaking the fountain adventure alone and ahead of the court — otherwise there would be abundant witnesses, as there are when he finally defeats the seneschal. A further irony is that he is saved from the portcullises, which had killed many men (l.1100), by leaning forward to grasp Esclados from behind (ll.938-41). Whilst Lunete later puts the best gloss she can on Yvain's pursuit by referring to his 'hardemant' (l.1708), Laudine more understandably construes it as murder (ll.1235f.; in fact, of course, the fatal blow is not struck from behind).

In short, Yvain's relentless hunting down of Esclados (note the antithesis *sagemant/folemant* at ll.933-34) in order to allay his anxiety about Kay's taunts, his denial of mercy to his defeated victim, his attempted assault from behind (if only for the theft of a token) all run counter to the rules of warfare set out in canon law and a variety of legal texts. Yvain's adventure perfectly illustrates John of Salisbury's complaint in his *Policraticus* Bk.8, ch.15 that by *temeritas* is incited 'violence, and the goad of vengeance by violence, like a blazing torch of hatred and war; the consequences are contempt for justice, violation of law and disquieting convulsion of public stability' (see 6, p.391). Equally illegitimate are Yvain's usurping of con-stituted authority to initiate hostilities, his promotion of self-interest by his clandestine departure from court, and his neglect of the requirement of a formal challenge at the fountain (on the role of the Dameisele Sauvage, see above p.29). The hero's moral insensitivity is further illustrated by his thoughts at the interment of the man he has killed. He strains to obtain permission to view 'la procession et le cors' (l.1274), but the narrator comments:

> *Mes* il n'avoit antancion
> N'au cors n'a la procession;
> Qu'il vossist qu'il fussent tuit ars,
> Si li eüst costé mil mars.
> Mil mars? Voire, par foi, trois mile.
> *Mes* por la dame de la vile
> Que il voloit veoir, le dist.
> (ll.1275-81)

He grieves that the body is committed to the earth without his having been able to snatch any token of his triumph (ll.1341-45). Is not Yvain in danger of being seen, to borrow words from John of Salisbury, as 'accursed with malice' (*malitiae exsecratus*) rather than 'devoted to true knightly service' (*ad legitimam militiam consecratus*)? The introduction to *Yvain* extolled the 'cortois morz' above the 'vilains vis'. The hero's achievement is now evoked in an ironic manipulation of these words which completely controverts the commendation of the prologue:

> Mes ore est mes sire Yvains sire
> Et li morz est toz obliez.
> Cil, qui l'ocist, est mariez
> An sa fame, et ansanble gisent,
> Et les janz aimment plus et prisent
> Le vif, qu'onques le mort ne firent.
>
> (ll.2164-69)

However much or little we have been coming to doubt Yvain's chivalry, we do so now. This apparent affirmation of the hero's good fortune contains an unmistakable intertextual reference to the marriage of Edipus and Jocasta in the *Roman de Thèbes*:

> Li dueus del rei est obliez,
> Cil qui mort l'a est coronez
> Et la reine a moillier prent.
>
> (*Roman de Thèbes*, ll.447-49)

The texts exhibit other parallels, too: the aphorism that women are easily led and the pleasing advice from the barons which confirms the private wishes of their mistress, who needs a defender. Success is only apparent. Yvain, who was so preoccupied with *ansaingnes veraies*, visible tokens, still hankers after the outward show of the tournaments. The love he has conquered is soon to change to hate. In both love and chivalry Yvain lacks the maturity to fulfil his responsibilities and maintain his good fortune. After his exile, a voluntary departure from court undertaken in a quite different spirit from his earlier escape, Yvain's chivalry undergoes a conspicuous transformation, the contrasts being pointed up by recognizable inversions of earlier themes (e.g. humility, mercy, punctuality). This new chivalry or *nova militia*, associated with the lion, will be examined in a later chapter.

The first part of *Yvain* is notable for the deployment of varied notions of chivalry all of which are subsequently transcended by the hero's reformed knighthood as the Chevalier au Lion. Calogrenant represents a vacuous knight-errantry, divorced from any ethical or practical basis, which, exercised by so ineffectual a warrior, attracts nothing but the contempt of the fountain knight (ll.540ff.). For this reason, apparently, and exceptionally (ll.572ff.), Calogrenant is allowed to escape. The rueful victim tells his story, years later, as a topic of entertainment rather than as the subject of a complaint requiring redress, but the headstrong Yvain is blinded to the incongruity of the offence and the exorbitant retribution which he exacts from Esclados. Calogrenant's tale is not 'de cuer antandu' and the ensuing vendetta illustrates as well as could be done that senseless waste of life among the nobility which led to increasing attempts to proscribe the feud in all but extreme cases, including the restricting of the degrees of paternity which might justify involvement. Esclados, eminently 'cortois' (ll.1288ff.) dies and is succeeded by a man who fails to meet his obligations — a 'vilains vis'?

Kay combines uncourtly *fanfaronnade* (cf. Yvain's parody of him at ll.632ff.) with malicious slander, acting as an *agent provocateur* in this instance, but more generally as a spur to action in a court where complacency and inertia are latent dangers (as is perhaps indicated by Arthur's initial withdrawal from the festivities — the incipient *roi fainéant*?). In goading Yvain with taunts about an early and solitary departure (which he does not expect to take place) Kay unwittingly echoes decisions which the hero has already taken. His intervention is ironical, strengthening rather than weakening Yvain's resolve, but it is also destructive, for his sarcasm upholds the hollowness of external codes of behaviour, unthinkingly applied, to which Yvain will fall victim in his relentless pursuit of Esclados in order to appease Kay. It is difficult to decide whether behind Kay's calumnies there lies an apprehension that the hero's mission is ill advised. On arriving at the fountain Kay once again condemns Yvain's empty boasts, remarking that 'Mout est hardiz, qui vanter s'ose / de ce, *dont autre ne l'alose*' (ll.2187f.).

Is the mission of revenge really praiseworthy — if it is 'properly understood'? However this may be, Kay's disquisition on the *mauvais* and the *preu* is easier to interpret. The *mauvais* is right to praise himself, for no one else will do it for him, whereas the truly *preu* would be embarrassed to hear his own praises sung. This alerts us to the problem of chivalric reputation. Yvain will not be content with the chivalric *coutume* maintained by Esclados, but will pursue the public spectacle of the tournaments in search of 'pris', renown, rather than service (*militia*). Only much later as the pseudonymous Knight of the Lion will he conceal his real prowess by declaring incognito to Laudine 'ne sui gueires renomez' (l.4620). Whilst Kay helps us, therefore, to discern some of the strands of chivalric fame, he himself is no more effectual than Calogrenant and suffers the same fate (*honte*) — he is knocked backwards out of the saddle and loses his horse (ll.2240ff.).

Gawain appears as something of a chivalric butterfly (see Busby, *20*). His chivalry is inseparable from the service of women. His flirtatious liaison with Lunete shows him characteristically promising more than he can deliver: 'Ma dameisele! Je vos doing / et a mestier et sanz besoing / un tel chevalier con je sui. / Ne me changiez ja por autrui, / se amander ne vos cuidiez. / Je sui vostre, et vos soiiez / d'ore an avant ma dameisele!' (ll.2433-39). When Lunete seeks a champion to defend her against the charge of treason, she seeks Gawain in vain, for he has left court to rescue the Queen who has been abducted (ll.3703ff.). Similarly, the victims of Harpin de la Montaigne are unable to apprise him of their misfortune because he is still absent from court (ll.3905ff.). The allusions to events of the *Lancelot* (see *Yvain* ll.3706ff., 3918ff., 4740ff.) neatly point up the dilemma caused by promises, particularly the *don contraignant* (on this see Frappier, *34* and Ménard, *63*), which inevitably create a conflict of duties. There is perhaps, too, an implied comparison of Gawain and Lancelot within the framework of courtly love. Even more problematic is Gawain's unavailability to help the younger sister of Noire Espine, for here the 'autre afere' (l.4770) which Gawain has undertaken is the defence of the elder sister who is manifestly in the wrong.

How discriminating, therefore, is his chivalry? The narrator refers ironically to the elder sister as 'cele, qui estoit seüre / del meillor chevalier del monde' (ll.4790f.): in the eyes of the younger sister Gawain is now replaced by the Knight of the Lion 'qui met sa painne a conseillier / celes, qui d'aïe ont mestier' (ll.4819f.). Yvain becomes a surrogate for Gawain, whilst transcending the latter's unreflecting chivalry. He recognizes at once the legitimacy of the younger sister's claims in the inheritance dispute (ll.5104-06), just as Arthur himself does (ll.5928-30), and although all his exploits are in the service of women (a reflection of his guilt at his abandonment of Laudine, who is defenceless?), they are based on a clear perception of justice. Gawain, as if in deference to the fact that the girl he champions 'tort a / vers sa seror trop an apert' (ll.5884-85) and 'par lui desresnier voldroit / la querele, ou ele n'a droit' (ll.5887-88) (cf. Arthur's clear recognition of this, ll.5909-11), arrives at court in disguise and lodges outside the town. Indeed, he early on (ll.4733-36) instructs the elder sister to conceal his identity.

The theme of identity is treated as a paradox. The Knight of the Lion is celebrated, but his identity unknown, whilst his opponent is apparently a stranger, though in reality celebrated at court. Reputation may rest on what a knight does or who he is. In the end the Knight of the Lion and the son of King Urien are made whole, there is a coalescence of action and essence which is denied to Gawain. Despite the narrator's strenuous efforts to present Yvain and Gawain as absolute equals, the inescapable fact is that Gawain bears final responsibility for the combat and for prolonging it. At last, his patience exhausted, Arthur threatens the elder sister with pronouncing her knight defeated (ll.6416f.). Only in terms of physical prowess are the two combatants truly equal. Yvain is not recognized because his lion has slipped away; he makes no attempt deliberately to conceal his identity. It is Gawain's careful disguise which alone compels the two friends to fight by preventing recognition. The blindness of love and hate, as depicted in the significant rhetorical elaboration of the combat, serves to remind us of the futility of knightly valour when divorced from a discriminating purpose. Consistently throughout the romance Yvain declines to criticize

Gawain and maintains his loyalty unimpaired as if to atone for
his former pride in seeking to pre-empt the fountain adventure
in which Gawain would have taken precedence. This humility,
however characteristic of Yvain's reorientated chivalry, cannot
conceal the weakness of Gawain's position and his moral
blindness. After the combat Gawain freely acknowledges that if
the fighting had continued, Yvain 'm'eüst mort / par sa proesce
et par le tort / celi qui m'avoit an chanp mis' (ll.6345-47). No
comparable confession leaves, or could leave, Yvain's lips.

In addition, of course, Gawain's chivalry is associated with
the tournaments, for it is the attraction of 'les tornoiemanz
ongier' (l.2504) which forms the central argument in his appeal
to Yvain to request leave from Laudine. Whilst the Church was
implacably opposed to tournaments as ritualized homicide (they
were banned at the Lateran Councils of 1139 and 1179, with
denial of Christian burial as a penalty) and secular authorities
also grew alarmed by the squandering of resources which they
occasioned, tournaments had their value as competitive displays
which stimulated professional skills, engendered a certain *esprit
de corps*, and attracted patronage. Success in the tourney, therefore, inevitably increased individual prestige, but it did little for
the common weal or *publica utilitas*. Gawain's arguments are
entirely self-interested: 'Gardez, que an vos ne remaigne, / biaus
conpainz! nostre conpaignie, / qu'an moi ne faudra ele mie'
(ll.2510-12). The narrator knows well that Gawain will not
willingly release Yvain (ll.2668-69) and so it happens that
Gawain 'le fist tant demorer, / que trestoz li anz fu passez / et de
l'autre an aprés assez' (ll.2674-76). It is, we may feel, a rueful
conscience at the power of this male *compagnonnage* which best
explains why Yvain is led to the service exclusively of women.
The tournaments remained pre-eminently the favoured venues
of the *juvenes* (see Duby, *29*), the unemployed of the twelfth
century with their fortunes still to make. Yvain is emphatically
no longer one of 'les jeunes'. He has come into a rich inheritance
and correspondingly serious responsibilities as defender of the
fountain, yet in his immaturity he cannot make the break with
the existence of the *juvenes* and Gawain has no desire to see him
make it.

There is, consequently, an element of irresponsibility and of egocentricity in the contrasted notions of chivalry displayed in the first part of *Yvain*. It is often pointed out that the story ends in Laudine's lands, as if to underline her autonomy. It is equally noteworthy that it is she who plays final host to the knight whose chivalry transcends that of Arthur's court. How seriously, then, should we take her? This leads us to our next chapter.

4. Omnia vincit amor?

'Love conquers all things'? Both the nature and function of love in *Yvain* are sources of critical disagreement. Traditionally-minded readers, brought up to believe that all Chrétien's romances treat of the ideal co-ordination of love and chivalry, insist that the love theme is indispensable to the moral and ideological texture of the work (see Noble, *65*). Others have seen in Laudine an illustration of Nietzsche's dictum that it is impossible to fathom a woman's depths — she has none (cf. Lefay-Toury, *59*, pp.203f.). A further option has been to see the amatory matter as the tongue-in-cheek elaboration of a literary fiction, which is ironically grafted onto the chivalry theme with the intention of producing a burlesque of courtly ideology (cf. Bogdanow, *17*).

The problems start with the 'prologue' and Chrétien's paradoxical contention that his contemporaries travesty love with their insincere protestations. The claim raises a number of difficult questions. Are the references directed at 'literary' love, promulgated by the poets, or at contemporary *mores*? Is the criticism levelled at the eroticism celebrated by *joculatores* and reflected in the *fabliaux*, or is it a token of Chrétien's lack of sympathy with the doctrines of love publicized by the troubadours? Actually, there is a similar complaint in a poem by one of the most famous troubadours, whose work Chrétien certainly drew on, Bernart de Ventadorn (see Appendix), so that Chrétien may be imitating, rather than criticizing, Provençal poetry! Or is he, perhaps, expressing pique at the reception given to his previous treatment of love (in *Erec*, *Cligés* or *Lancelot*)? — the *reprise* of the complaint later in *Yvain* coincides with the portrait of a young girl reading to her parents from 'ùn romanz, ne sai de cui' (l.5366), possibly a sly allusion to his own work. Others might see in Chrétien's remarks an indication that the society of his time had not succeeded in integrating love and chivalry in a stable ideal.

If we take the feudal analogy of the vassalic relationship to be central to the conception of 'Courtly Love' or *fin' amors* (see Boase, *16*), it rapidly becomes evident that courtly ideology is itself problematic. The woman's inspiration of love-service in one or more knights is easy to celebrate in terms of the emotions it inspires — for instance, in lyric poetry — but it is difficult to translate into action, still more to depict in narrative. The whole notion of success or achievement, the resolution of a productive tension in the man, remains ambiguous (see Ferrante, *32* and Halligan, *44*). If the moral value of *fin' amors* resides in aspiration itself, then the lady need never be 'possessed' and, indeed, ought not to be, since this would be to terminate the educative process. Such a Platonic strain, whilst undoubtedly present in some poets, is conspicuously absent from others. If, on the other hand, aspiration is to lead to fulfilment, does it then follow that the lady (*dompna*) should be unmarried? The persistent view that she is, on the contrary, married and that 'Courtly Love' is by definition adulterous must surely depend on, more than anything else, Andreas Capellanus's dictum that love is impossible in marriage, which is probably a playful inversion of the Church's view that adultery is possible within it! At any rate, it is illogical to identify *non*-conjugal love with *extra*-conjugal love (see Press, *72*). Adultery was strictly condemned in the married woman because of inheritance problems, but not in the man, when no issue of patrimony was at stake. In the twelfth century men frequently repudiated wives when this served the interest of the patrimony. Marriage was essentially endogamous, that is, confined within the clan. The association of marriage with dynastic interests and patrimony made it natural that spontaneous love should be depicted as non-conjugal (see Duby, *30* and *31*).

Against this background, Chrétien has made Yvain's love for Laudine just about as ambiguous as could be. First, the hero falls in love with the widow whose husband he has just slain — there are reminiscences of Oedipus and Jocasta as well as the Widow of Ephesus. Second, Chrétien subjects his hero to the stylized, Ovidian symptoms of Amor along lines familiar to anyone who had frequented the schools of northern France and suggests the possibility of a typically Ovidian strategy, the taking, through carefully prepared oratory and the services of a handmaiden (*ancilla*), of a woman who *feigns* reluctance (see *Ars Amatoria* I, 265ff.). Third, the relationship of Yvain and Laudine is depicted in terms which humorously reflect many of the images and themes of the troubadour Bernart de Ventadorn, who seems to have been a poetic rival to Chrétien (see Appendix). Finally, the relationship is situated in a context of power politics, *Machtpolitik*, which impels Laudine to marry again in order to secure the defence of her fountain and territory, a defence which her own vassals are too cowardly to undertake. The marriage of Yvain and Laudine is thus presented as a rather disconcerting combination of emotion and practical necessity, freedom and compulsion, desire and *raison d'état*. They love each other (do they do so freely?), but at the same time recognize marriage as the only way out of an impasse — Yvain must secure proof of his victory at the fountain in order to satisfy Kay, whilst Laudine must enlist a new defender of her lands. Love as a spontaneous emotion is incorporated in what look suspiciously like an expedient, a *mariage de convenance*. Like the chivalric theme, the love plot gets off to a somewhat shaky start.

Typically, in this romance at least, the emergence of love is associated with deception. Yvain announces to Lunete during his imprisonment in a room in Laudine's castle that he would fain see 'la procession et le cors' (l.1274), though the narrator assures us that he would have paid to have the funeral mourners burned, so little is his real concern for Esclados's obsequies (ll.1275-81). What he is interested in is 'la dame de la vile'. With characteristic impetuosity Yvain thinks of rushing out to take the grief-stricken widow by the hands, but is dissuaded by Lunete from the temptation 'de folie faire' (l.1308), 'd'outrage feire' (l.1322b). The repetition of *folie* and *outrage* underscores the hero's impulsiveness and Lunete's comments evoke at once his pursuit of Esclados and the danger of carrying over his chivalric imprudence into the amatory sphere. Whilst the apologists of *fin' amors* recognize as axiomatic its lack of *mesure*, Lunete declares: '... qui se desroie et sormainne / et d'outrage feire se painne, / quant il an a et eise et leu, / je l'apel plus mauvés que preu' (ll.1322a-d). Nevertheless, Lunete's promise of 'granz biens' (l.1316) and 'mout grant avantage' (l.1321) indicate that collusion has already begun. From this moment we realize that Yvain is not only literally a prisoner in the castle, but is also soon to be imprisoned in a further, para-doxical and metaphorical sense. The transition from a situation in which he *cannot*, to one in which he *will not*, escape is characteristic of the skill and dexterity with which Chrétien combines psychological motivation (however playful) with a narrative composition which is frequently complex and unpre-dictable. It also shows him manipulating the literary conventions of courtly literature in a typically ironic manner: the conceit of love's prison (ll.1922ff.) is undercut by the reality of the hero's literal imprisonment in Lunete's chamber.

The fire of love is kindled even as the ashes of a former union are committed to the earth. Such a coincidence, in its ambi-valence and distastefulness, formed the stock in trade of much medieval anti-feminist satire and is here embodied in a striking oxymoron: Yvain finds Laudine 'si bele iriee' (l.1490), 'so beautiful in her sorrow'. This is continued in the curiously bifocal portrait of the grieving widow (ll.1462-90), where each part of her physiognomy is successively the centre of a violent gesture and then of the hero's admiring appreciation. Since it might be considered offensive that the hero should determine 'in cold blood' to woo the bereaved lady of the fountain, he must be handed over to the power of Love, which will direct his actions. The impetuosity of the knight is now converted into the extra-vagance of the courtly lover in a passage dense with conceits and paradoxes which amply display Chrétien's love of dialectic (ll.1339-1405). Yvain is now detained by the twin forces of Honte and Amors: the need to secure credibility at court through visible tokens of victory at the fountain, and submission to the power of Love, which it is 'felenie et traïson' (l.1446) to resist. The smarting caused by Kay's taunts (ll.1354-55) and Yvain's impetuous desire for the woman he has widowed are glossed over by being presented as duty, according to the dictates of love and honour. Military and amatory metaphors are mingled, following a tradition which had a long history since Ovid's 'Every lover is a soldier' ('militat omnis amans', *Amores* I,ix,1) and 'Love is a kind of warfare' ('militiae species amor est', *Ars Amatoria*, 2,233). Love appears as an aggressive force ('s'a tote sa proie [= booty] acoillie' (l.1359), 'qu'Amors s'est tote a lui randue' (l.1377)), which nevertheless bears sweetness (cf. *radoucist* l.1357, *doucemant* l.1368). The courtly metaphor of love's wound which deteriorates in the presence of the doctor (ll.1371-77) ironically recalls the wound of Esclados which bleeds in the presence of the murderer (ll.1178ff.). Another common conceit, love striking the heart through the eyes (l.1368; see Cline, *22*) maintains the imagery of physical assault, which is designed to produce the central irony of revenge being taken on the avenger.

More important than the revenge which is sought by Esclados's barons (l.1058) is the way in which Laudine (in most of the MSS she appears simply as *la dame*) obtains revenge (ll.1362, 1364, 1366) for her husband's death through the power of love, which overpowers him who 'aimme la rien, qui plus le het' (l.1361). Yvain, who is on a quest of vengeance, now falls victim to a new form of revenge. The parallelism of the military and amatory metaphors may already suggest that the hero's qualifications and status as a lover are no better than those as a knight. At this point, therefore, Chrétien interposes a passage (ll.1378-1405) defending Love's discrimination here against the background of its baser promiscuity, an idea introduced by the etymological play on *ostel*, *oste*, *oster*, *ost*. This is naturally also a defence of the hero, whose conduct might otherwise appear dubious, and a reminder of the polemic against false lovers. As in the 'prologue', *Amors* remains an ethically ambiguous force. The trenchant paradox of loving one's enemy (elaborated in ll.1450-61, *amer-haïr*, *ami-anemi*), with its ironic echo of a Christian injunction, reveals, as so often in this romance, Chrétien's delight in undercutting metaphors by supplying literal equivalents: 'Ançois amerai m'anemie: / que je ne la doi pas haïr, / se je ne vuel Amor traïr' (ll.1450-52).

Typically, the problems of a difficult narrative transition are

made to evaporate in a playful, casuistical debate. It is one thing
to love one's enemy, but how shall the enemy return that love if
a serious injury has already been sustained (ll.1430ff.)? In a
poem of Bernart de Ventadorn the poet examines the hopeless-
ness of loving passionately where he cannot be loved, yet love
descends where it pleases (cf. *Yvain* ll.1395ff.) and if it makes
him love, why should it not also possess his lady? — *car Amors
vens tota chauza*, 'love conquers all things' (see Appendix).
Chrétien, whilst constantly inspired by the *tensos* or disputes of
troubadour lyrics, now falls back on a classical tag which has
endured from Virgil to Verdi — *semper mutabile est femina*,
'fame a plus de mil corages' (l.1436). Thus, by a process of
courtly ratiocination Yvain can overturn his earlier objection
('Por fol me puis tenir / quant je vuel ce que ja n'avrai',
ll.1428-29) and through a belief about the nature of women conclude 'Si sui mout fos, qui m'an despoir' (l.1440). The hope is,
of course, ironic, since by the same token the lady can change
back again, turning love to hate (cf. l.2564).

Women's fickleness, a convention of antifeminist satire, is
taken up again in lines 1640-44, a passage strongly reminiscent
of Ovid, and also of Bernart de Ventadorn in a poem which has
a special relevance to Chrétien (see Appendix). This increases the
ambiguity of the wooing of Laudine. Do we have here the taking
by storm of a lady whose reluctance is only feigned, in the
manner of Ovid? Or are we presented with a picture of courtly
submission, the hero now being humbled by the power of love
and offering homage to an imperious mistress or *dompna*? The
hero's conception of what appears to be a passionate love for the
widow of the man he has just slain left Chrétien with the dual
problem of narrative plausibility and ethical decorum. He
invokes both chivalric and amatory codes to explain how
Yvain's physical imprisonment in the castle becomes a psychological one and draws heavily on Ovid as ironist and on the
courtly motifs of Bernart de Ventadorn.

Equally redolent of literary burlesque is the presentation of
Yvain to Laudine as a *fin amant*. Through the verbal and logical
skill of an astute *entremetteuse* the unrestrained grief of a
sorrowing widow is changed to the decorously restrained

curiosity of a nubile, young woman, but Yvain does not yet have
the measure of this change. This is perhaps not surprising, for
the change in Laudine ('Ez vos ja la dame changiee', l.1749) is
still ambiguous. Is it produced by a surge of natural feeling overcoming the perversity of her sex (l.1644) or is it the reaction of a
haughty, deeply offended *dompna* (see Press, *73*) who has been
won over by Lunete's specious logic in such a way 'que droit,
san et reison i trueve' (l.1774)? Just as Chrétien draws virtuoso
semantic effects from the interplay of military and amatory
metaphors, so the contest of syllogistic logic and natural instinct
is used to burlesque both nature and reason. Expedience (the
defence of the fountain), reason (the victor is necessarily
superior, cf. *prover* in ll.1611, 1704), curiosity (can there be a
knight so worthy as the dead fountain knight?), decorum (a
noble lady should not grieve overlong), noble prejudice (Yvain is
King Urien's son), respect for the *bona fides* of her counsellor,
impatience ('Cist termes est trop lons assez', l.1832) all coalesce
to kindle a flame 'aussi con la busche, qui fume, / tant que la
flame s'i est mise, / que nus ne sofle ne atise' (ll.1778-80). The
hint of desire in this image leaves the nature of Laudine's newly
discovered inclination ambivalent. There is a delightful irony in
the way that she achieves conviction by appropriating the logic
which she had earlier rejected as 'desreison' (l.1710, cf. l.1701)
on the lips of her servant, and 'proving' (l.1773), in a miniature
cross examination in her mind, that the defendant should be
acquitted. But this constant intersection of reason and emotion,
physical realities and metaphorical conceits, moral concerns and
sentimental impulses, produces a vertiginous uncertainty in the
audience. Is the prison now evoked by Lunete a trap?

In a passage in which the word *prison* occurs eight times
(ll.1910-42) we are led to reflect on how far this nascent union is
based on freedom of action and how far on force of circumstances. Are Yvain and Laudine the prisoners of external codes,
of practical necessity, or of literary conventions? Yvain, who
dare not anticipate such a favourable reception as he in fact
obtains, is afraid — the *traductio* or repetition of *peur*
(ll.1950ff.) reminds us of Andreas Capellanus's 'The lover is
always apprehensive' (*amorosus semper est timorosus*) and

Bernart de Ventadorn's poem in which he trembles before his lady like a leaf before the wind and is forced to remind himself that the lady is not a bear or a lion intent on killing him (cf. *Yvain* ll.1966f., see Appendix).

Laudine's request that the knight who slew her husband explain how he has come to be 'si dontez' (l.2014) — a situation which parallels the similar change in Laudine from the grieving of an apparently distraught widow to the willing submission to her lady-in-waiting — calls forth an exchange which, exploiting the figure of *anadiplosis* (reprise of immediately preceding terms; ll.2017ff.), presents with flawless rhetoric a miniature catechism of the courtly lover. Yvain kneels, hands clasped, in a posture which reproduces the homage of a feudal vassal to his lord (see Jonin, *58*), the juridical connotations of which (see Ourliac, *67*) are ironically at variance with the *traïson* of which Yvain initially stands accused. He will thank the lady for whatever action she is pleased to take (ll.1975ff.), recognizing the courtly doctrine of grace, and will do her will. The conversation ends with a reminder of one of a vassal's customary obligations, war service. Yvain's agreement to defend the fountain produces the speedy response 'Sachiez donc, bien acordé somes' (l.2036) and the narrator's laconic observation 'Einsi sont acordé briemant' (l.2037). It is obvious that the foundations of this union are shaky from more than one point of view and that the audience desires the satisfaction of knowing that Laudine truly loves Yvain, an assurance which has been conspicuous up till now by its absence.

It is characteristic of Chrétien that he withholds this information until the last minute, just as he withholds the lady of the fountain's name. The seneschal, ironically unaware that the candidate is the man who has murdered Esclados, recommends his acceptance as the lady's new husband. The narrator slyly indicates that all the negotiations are merely *pro forma*, so far as the lady is concerned:

> Si se fet proiier de son buen,
> Tant que aussi con maugré suen
> Otroie ce, qu'ele feïst,

Se chascuns li contredeïst.

(ll.2109-12; cf. 2137-40)

Whilst the audience is thus satisfied as to the sincerity of
Laudine's volte-face, it is led to look sceptically at the narrator's
rhetoric, for if both Yvain and Laudine do not always say what
they mean or mean what they say (deception is inseparable from
the love plot in this romance), is there any reason to suppose that
the narrator's utterances are exempt from the ambivalence and
irony of courtly rhetoric? As in *Cligés*, Chrétien burlesques
deliberative oratory as either mere rationalization or as a substitute for action.

Such is the case with Gawain's exhortation to the hero to
depart for the tournaments (ll.2484-2538). Here the probative
value of three courtly commonplaces of love is evacuated by
their absurd incongruity with Yvain's circumstances and by
Gawain's own admission that he would not, in his friend's
position, be anxious to implement them (ll.2527-38). Gawain's
arguments purport to fill a vacuum in the chivalric life left by
marriage, but it is the peculiar nature of the new union to be so
associated with the defence of the fountain as to abhor such a
vacuum. The first argument contrasts *anpirier* and *amander*.
But Yvain has been married for only a week and there is not the
slightest indication that any deterioration in his chivalric
reputation will take place! On the contrary, the necessity of
defending the fountain supports the opposite inference. His
succession as fountain knight demonstrates his clear superiority
to all the men of Laudine's court and his duties would seem to
preclude the *recreantise* or lethargy which afflicted Erec in
Chrétien's first romance. The cornerstone of courtly love ideology, 'Amander doit de bele dame, / qui l'a a amie ou a fame'
(ll.2489-90), seems solidly located in a relationship which
involves Yvain's service to his lady as her liege-man. The second
argument — 'Or primes doit vostre pris croistre' (l.2499) —
seems gratuitous when addressed to a knight who has just
defeated Kay, avenged a kinsman, and succeeded to important
new territories. Gawain's conception of 'Celui, qui de neant
anpire / quant il est del reaume sire' (ll.2497-98) is theoretically

in flat contradiction to Yvain's new office and its duties. The old saw 'assez songe, qui ne se muet' (1.2507) has no relevance to a knight committed henceforth to the defence of the fountain, and the appeal to a romanticized myth of chivalric glamour in the tournaments is a backward-looking evocation of the *compagnonnage* of the two knights. After this somewhat distorted account of the chivalry topos Gawain resorts to an epicurean argument concerning the experience of love itself:

> Biens adoucist par delaiier,
> Et plus est buens a essaiier
> Uns petiz biens, quant il delaie,
> Qu'uns granz, que l'an adés essaie.
>
> (ll.2515-18)

This proposition, which is immediately followed by a reminiscence of Ovid's *Ars amatoria* 3, 573, exemplifies the presentation of love in terms of contemporary literary fiction. *Biens adoucist par delaiier* has been lifted from Chrétien's own lyric poem 'D'Amors, qui m'a tolu a moi', where it functions as an intertextual reference of some complexity. Chrétien's poem, which like his romance contains a complaint about deceivers in love and the motif of the gift of the lover's heart, is part of a poetic polemic between Chrétien and the troubadour poets Raimbaut d'Aurenga and Bernart de Ventadorn, who all wrote poems on the separation of the lover and his lady, but argued quite different solutions, Chrétien's being the most optimistic (see Zai, *89*, pp.92-96). When viewed in this literary context, Gawain's words take on a threefold significance: (i) his advice is fashioned after a consciously literary model or pose, underscoring the notion of roles which is important in this romance; (ii) an irony is produced by the fact that his words evoke beside the now safely established Yvain two Provençal lyrics which emphasize the lover's discontented separation from his lady, thus providing an ironic anticipation of Yvain's fate; (iii) Chrétien's own lyric, from which Gawain borrows a line, provides a contrasting optimism which will shortly be belied by the narrator's prediction that hope will play Yvain false (ll.2658ff.). This web of intertextual references brilliantly generates a tension between the possibilities of unhappy separation and optimistic persistence. On which side will Yvain fall? Or perhaps we should say: which role will he adopt?

Leave is now obtained from Laudine with a variation on the theme of 'I could not love thee, Dear, so much / loved I not Honour more'. The *congié* (the word is repeated five times, with ironic echoes of l.1527) is granted after what amounts to the use of the *don contraignant*, that is the exacting of an open-ended promise (ll.2549ff.; see Frappier, *34* and Ménard, *63*). Again Laudine's freedom of manœuvre is limited, but she indicates plainly that if Yvain outstays the period of leave, 'l'amors devandra haïne' (l.2564). In what is a clear testing of the hero's maturity and stability a remarkable naïveté emerges. In an ironic echo of Laudine's exclamation at line 1832, Yvain protests that the period of leave is too long. Yet, his eagerness to return is already qualified by his reference to the possible *essoines* (impediments) of *malage* and *prison* (ll.2590-91). It is possible to doubt his good faith here, but Laudine's gift of the magic ring definitively removes any physical hindrance to his prompt return — provided, of course, that he acts as an 'amanz verais et leaus'. This brings into relief the hero's individual responsibility (see Cooper, *25*, pp.133-34). After Yvain's *breve gaudium*, short-lived bliss indeed, the impending *peripeteia* or reversal is such an obvious narrative necessity that Chrétien makes not the slightest attempt to surprise his audience or to elaborate the hero's fault. The legalistic atmosphere of Yvain's final reconciliation with Laudine is foreshadowed by the use of a legal formula which has already appeared in the legal context of Esclados's complaint to Calogrenant — 'Mout a anviz trovera mes / A sa dame *triues ne pes*' (ll.2665-66, cf. l.516).

After Yvain's transgression he is denounced by a maiden from Laudine's court (ll.2721-73). It is striking that the medieval translators of the *Yvain* (see Hunt, *55*) refocus her speech on the theme of Yvain's status as a knight, whereas in Chrétien it is exclusively his status as a lover that is impugned. Yvain is not a 'verais amerre', he does not understand 'come li amant font' (l.2760), he is a thief (see the *traductio* of *anbler* and *cuer*, ll.2728-45). In short, to borrow words from the 'prologue', he appears to be one of those 'qui rien n'an santent, / dient qu'il aimment, mes il mantent' (ll.25-26). Again, we note how the characters, here the *dameisele*, formulate their ideas in literary terms. The denunciation centres on the exchange of hearts (*cuers/cors*) topos. Whilst the role of memory is evoked only three times (*oblianz, ressovenir, remanbra*) the images of traitor, robber, cheat crowd together: *desleal, traïtor, mançongier, jeingleor, lerre, larron, soduire*. In other words, Yvain presented a false image of himself. His simple error in overstaying his leave is now regarded as symptomatic of his true nature. It is this conversion of an act of omission into a definitive trait of character which has led some critics to see here the 'overreaction' of a lofty and imperious *dompna*, though they perhaps forget Laudine's extreme vulnerability as a precipitately remarried widow who has buried an apparent paragon of courtliness (whose status is undercut by his red hair!). We might, of course, construe this single-minded concentration on Yvain's failure as a courtly lover as being essentially determined by the courtly image of the *fin amant* which he himself chose to present to Laudine.

It creates, nonetheless, an awkward problem. How can Yvain's chivalric adventures in the second part of the romance possibly be seen as redeeming him *qua* lover and what grain of evidence is provided in the *sicut ante* ending to suggest that Laudine receives him as a lover at all?

The difficulties of assessing the ethical value of the love theme are exacerbated by the contrast of Yvain's friendship with Gawain. We may be put in mind of Oliver Goldsmith's distinction of friendship as 'disinterested commerce between equals' and love as 'an abject intercourse between tyrants and slaves'. Certainly, the friendship of the two knights is greatly prized — by themselves and by the narrator who comments 'Qu'amors, qui n'est fausse ne fainte, / est precieuse chose et sainte' (ll.6051-52). There has long been a consensus of the critics that Chrétien could not allow Yvain to defeat Gawain in their incognito combat without damaging the equity of their friendship. It is also noteworthy that Yvain never exhibits the

slightest trace of resentment towards Gawain for the part played
by him in his own misfortunes. On the contrary, he is at pains
throughout the romance to serve Gawain and honour him (see,
for example, ll.3699ff., 3980ff., 4039ff., 4068ff., 4273ff.) and at
one point (ll.4071ff.) associates Gawain with God and the Virgin
in a trinity which binds him to fight against Harpin.

There is a sense in which Yvain acts as a surrogate for
Gawain, for all his adventures have as their goal the liberation of
women from oppression and of Gawain he says 'A s'aïe ne failli
onques / dameisele desconseilliee, / que ne li fust apareilliee'
(ll.3700-02). Their comparability in the chivalric sphere invites
examination of their relationship in the amatory sphere. The
paradoxical combat of the two friends near the end of the
romance, which associates *ami* with *anemi*, *amor* with *haïne*,
reminds us of Yvain's no less paradoxical relationship with
Laudine, originally described in the same terms (ll.1449-61) and
we are perhaps tempted to see in the final reconciliation of the
two knights, through the disclosure of identity, an anticipation
of the reunion of Yvain and his lady. Yet we have already seen
the difficulty of taking the latter episode entirely seriously. It
may be noted that Chrétien is careful, when describing the
wedding celebrations at Laudine's court, to allow Gawain his
own courtship (ll.2395ff.) whereby he offers service to Lunete,
as his *amie*, and expresses the hope that she will never give him
up for another. But Gawain, like Yvain, is 'prevented' from ful-
filling his obligations — without apparently incurring disappro-
bation! Are they both, then, comparable as *fins amanz*? Does
Chrétien really take love seriously at all? Does he not, in fact,
issue a warning against taking courtly rhetoric and smooth talk
too literally?

> Et çaus puet l'an nices clamer,
> Qui cuident, que les vuelle amer,
> Quant une dame est si cortoise,
> Qu'a un maleüreus adoise,
> Si li fet joie et si l'acole.
> Fos est liez de bele parole,
> Si l'a an mout tost amusé.

(ll.2459-65)

How far are Gawain and Yvain truly differentiated as knights and *fins amanz*? One might well hope to find a clear answer by examining Yvain's chivalric exploits. After his voluntary exile from court there are really only three further allusions to the love theme. When the hero is led by *avanture* (l.3490) to the fountain, his grief erupts in self-condemnation. Like the troubadours, he laments the loss of his *joie* (the word occurs six times) and also, more ironically, he revives the notion of *haïr*, this time in reference to his own attitude to himself. He is already repentant: 'Et qui ce pert par son mesfet, / n'est droiz que buene avanture et' (ll.3561-62). His guilt and the discovery of Lunete exclude any precipitate course of action such as raising the storm again. On his return to rescue Lunete, it is significant that Laudine is foremost in his mind, or rather, his heart (ll.4344ff.), and that the Ovidian imagery is maintained (ll.4348-51, cf. *Amores* 2, 9, 29-30; the whole poem is a fascinating commentary on the dialectic of love and repose), yet Yvain does not reveal his identity and avoids any attempt at reunion. Why? The incognito meeting with his wife seems to serve two purposes in respect of the dénouement: it allows Laudine to know *at first hand* the prowess of the Knight of the Lion and his embroilment with his mistress, thus increasing the likelihood of her supporting Lunete's suggested oath at the end, and, secondly, it enables Yvain, fully aware that his lady has this knowledge and has pity on him for the way he has been treated, to leave with some vestigial belief in the possibility that further adventures will help bring about her forgiveness of him.

But can we be sure that Yvain *does* undertake later adventures in such a belief? The answer to this question resides in a statement of seemingly irremediable ambiguity. Yvain tells Laudine that he cannot afford to tarry until he receives the forgiveness of his lady: 'Lors finera *mes travauz* toz' (l.4592). A connexion between his love and his chivalric exploits can only be established by taking *travauz* to indicate 'chivalric labours, exertions', but it is at least as probable that it means 'travail, troubles' (cf. the *pesance* and *ire* of l.4628, and *Cligés*, l.4576) in which case no connexion is established. At any rate, Yvain makes no attempt at reconciliation here, departing with a typical

lover's conceit (ll.4632-34). Is he, perhaps, discouraged by
Laudine's qualification that his lady has behaved badly 'se trop
n'eüst vers li mespris' (l.4598)? Or does he subscribe to Gawain's
theory that 'Biens adoucist par delaiier', which would certainly
be ironical? Does he now see his fault, not as simple forgetful-
ness, but as an exemplification of disordered chivalry which
must be replaced by a new image of social service and the
defence of the oppressed? In the reconciliation scene Yvain
declares 'Conparé ai mon fol savoir, / et je le dui bien conparer'
(ll.6782-83). Again, a crucial admission is left frustratingly
imprecise. Does *fol savoir* mean 'my misguided understanding
of chivalry'? Does *conparé* mean 'paid for (in suffering)' or
'expiated (by acts of public service)'? One can only conclude
that Chrétien had no desire to provide a clear-cut answer.

5. *Nobilis ira leonis* —
The Anger of the Noble Lion

'To bring in — God shield us! — a lion among ladies, is a most dreadful thing.' Bottom's words are an apt reminder of the traditional ferocity of the lion, which might be thought scarcely at home in a courtly romance, and of its illustration in Ovid's tale of Pyramus and Thisbe (*Metamorphoses*, 4, 55-166), which was the subject of a number of adaptations in Chrétien's day. The lion certainly cannot be dismissed as peripheral. Chrétien concludes his poem with 'Del Chevalier au lion fine / Crestiiens son romanz einsi' (ll.6814-15) — the title *Yvain* is an editorial superscription which merely has the convenience of being shorter. Yet the lion plays no part in the final episode of the romance (it receives a final cursory mention at l.6727), despite the fact that it is said to accompany the hero for the rest of his life (ll.3412-15, 3451-55, 5020-21).

'The Knight of the Lion' certainly suggests some form of symbiosis and on two occasions, it is true, Chrétien anthropomorphizes his ferocious beast. The first instance presents the grateful lion (reminiscent of counterparts in a variety of stories from Aulus Gellius to Alexander Nequam) which reacts to its rescue by the hero with tears and humility in a clear posture of submission (ll.3392-407). Shortly after, in an ironic manipulation of the gestures of Pyramus when he thinks Thisbe is dead, the lion attempts suicide with its master's sword, so great is its identification with the knight's fortunes (ll.3492-525). Perhaps, then, we should conclude that 'The Lyon is not so fierce as they paint him'. On the other hand, the traditional ferocity of the lion is several times alluded to in similes associated with military activity (ll.488, 3203-04) and the predatory nature of the beast is given prominence in the scene of forest life, which symbolizes the temporary subordination of *norreture* to *nature*. On another occasion, however, the lion is compared with a lamb (l.4012)!

The combination of ferocity and humility seems to suggest, therefore, a certain dualism in the lion. We begin by believing with Bottom 'there is not a more fearful wild-fowl than your lion living' and come to recognize with Theseus that it may be 'a very gentle beast, and of a good conscience'.

Hitherto, interpretations of the lion in *Yvain* have assumed that it is associated with Christ and its role is redemptive, or that it symbolizes justice and its significance is judicial (see Hunt, *57*). It is true that at Pesme Avanture Yvain is seen as a liberator comparable with the Messiah (ll.5780-83) and that many of his interventions receive legal justification, but it might also be pointed out that his involvement in Pesme Avanture is involuntary (the liberation of the captive silkworkers coming as a somewhat belated request, ll.5708-11), and that in the major legal episode — the inheritance dispute — the lion plays no part at all. Neither the christological nor judicial interpretation of the lion easily accommodates the prominent motif of *gratitude*.

The Patristic exegesis from which the religious symbolism of the lion is largely derived understandably lays little emphasis on the idea of service rendered by the lion, though, as the following example will show, it does not preclude it. The legend of St Mary the Egyptian does not seem to have been invoked by students of Chrétien's lion. The legend ultimately goes back to a Greek account by Sophronios (died c. 638), but also forms the subject of a number of Latin poems and, more importantly, of several Old French adaptations, the oldest of which is contemporary with Chrétien (see Dembowski, *2*; refs. to version 'T'). In this story the monk Zosimas goes out into the desert to administer communion, as he had promised, to the penitent prostitute Mary. Finding her dead, he wishes to bury her, but recognizes that he lacks the strength to do so. At this point 'Diex li tramist bon compaignon' (l.1417) in the shape of a lion, which emerges from the desert and licks the feet of the corpse ('Nes savoit altrement baisier', l.1422) and does obeisance to the monk: 'Signe faisait de l'obeïr / Et que il le voloit servir' (ll.1423-24). Zosimas is at first unenthusiastic and is only restrained from fleeing by the sight of the noble animal 'de si grant humilité / et tant soef com un agnel' (ll.1432-33, cf. *Yvain*, ll.4011-12). The 'beste mue' sees to the grave, but understandably cannot undertake the commendation of the penitent's soul. It therefore prepares to leave: 's'obedience ot akievee, / a terre s'est agenollié' (ll.1478-79). It then ambles off into the desert. Here, then, is an *a posteriori* argument for seeing in Yvain's lion the 'long arm of God'. And yet, it is precisely by entertaining such a view that we come to appreciate how Chrétien has playfully 'blocked' the traditional christological interpretation of the lion, as we shall now see.

First, despite its legendary virtues, the 'rex omnium animalium', 'animal omnium generosissimum', 'princeps omnium bestiarum', whose name means king, is first discovered by the hero in undignified distress, clearly getting the worst of an encounter with a fire-breathing serpent (ll.3347ff.). It is true that medieval encyclopaedists report the lion's great fear of fire, but the serpent is obviously less an incendiary device than a symbol of evil, as Yvain himself recognizes (ll.3357ff.). This potential Christ symbol is being held by the tail in desperate straits. Second, Yvain is motivated to assist the beast, not by any positive recognition of its virtues, but simply by pity for its plight in contending with such an obviously evil and venomous creature. Moreover, as he prepares to attack the serpent he envisages the possibility of having to fight against the lion afterwards (ll.3369-77), despite the compassion he feels for 'la beste jantil et franche'. The letter of the text inhibits any expectation that Yvain makes his decision confidently or recognizes in the lion any principle which has a moral claim to his help. Third, the reaction of the lion, when liberated, is neither to attack the hero, as he imagines it may, nor to leave him with mute relief, but to adopt a subservient rather than regal posture. This is a singularly domesticated lion and we may well reflect with Theseus 'I wonder if the lion be to speak'. This anthropopathic beast seems to have little of the transcendental about it. Chrétien was too learned to ignore the obvious possibilities presented by the lion for allegorical exploration and commentary and took the opportunity, it seems, to confound the *clergie* of his audience by frustrating their expectations. He does this by specifically alluding to the allegorized properties of the lion in the encyclo-

paedias and bestiaries and then 'blocking' them by ironic
inversion (cf. other examples in Haidu, *43*). Here are four
examples.

The apparently gratuitous detail that Yvain finally freed the
lion by cutting off a piece of its tail (ll.3382-87) responds to the
widespread view, following Pliny's *Natural History* VIII,19 (see
11, p.39), that 'Lions indicate their state of mind by means of
their tail' (cf. *Yvain*, ll.5532-33). The commonest property in the
bestiaries is the lion's habit of sleeping with its eyes open, a
detail which is allegorized as early as the *Physiologus* in the
motif of Christ's vigilance. What, then, does Chrétien make of
leo vigilans? — '... li lions ot tant de sans, / qu'il veilla et fu an
espans / del cheval garder, qui peissoit / l'erbe, qui petit
l'angreissoit' (ll.3481-84). Chrétien playfully reveals that it is not
its master that the lion keeps an eye on — the deliberate bathos
of the reference to the horse's meagre diet undercuts the
traditional associations of the vigilance motif. Another feature
of the lion in the bestiaries is its skill in eluding hunters by
obliterating its tracks with its tail, a custom which is then given a
christological interpretation. Chrétien inverts this by casting the
lion in the role of the hunter, seeking out its prey with the
instinct of a hunting dog (ll.3438ff.). Whereas Pliny describes
the lion as withdrawing contemptuously whilst in full view of the
pack and then proceeding at top speed when under cover of
brushwood, Chrétien makes it hunter and adjunct to the
huntsman. Finally, Pliny also initiates the tradition that the
lion's great strength resides in its breast ('vis summa in pectore').
Chrétien shows the lion intent on piercing its breast with its
master's sword (l.3519, cf. ll.3550-51) and this attempted suicide
must surely be a serious impediment to any specifically Christian
interpretation of the lion's role.

We return to the dualism of the lion: its ferocity and humility.
Whilst religious allegories show little concern with the former,
the judicial realm harbours few traces of the latter. The two
properties combine in the notion of reciprocity and it is this
recognition that puts us on the trail of a remarkably tenacious
tradition. Pliny notes (*Natural History* VIII,19) 'The lion alone
of wild animals shows mercy to suppliants; it spares persons

prostrated [*prostratis*] in front of it'. There follow two stories of grateful lions! Isidore of Seville, in his celebrated *Book of Etymologies* (XII,2,6) remarks that the lion shows mercy in a number of ways; it spares the 'prostrate', allows prisoners to return home, and does not attack a man unless hungry or injured. The crucial idea that the lion spares the defeated already contrasts vigorously with Yvain's initial conduct at the fountain and his relentless pursuit of the mortally wounded Esclados. It is taken up in a number of medieval encyclopaedias which commend the conduct of the lion to 'men who possess reason'. This particular property of the lion, when extended to men, is rapidly associated with the ideal of the Christian ruler, *rex justus et pius*.

The link with the *justus* is already provided by a number of classical writers. In Book Three of the *Tristia* Ovid hopes for merciful treatment from Augustus with the words 'The greater a man is, the more can his wrath be appeased: a noble spirit is capable of kindly impulses. For the noble lion [*magnanimo leoni*] 'tis enough to have overthrown his enemy; the fight is at an end when his foe is fallen' (see *12*, p.123). Ovid contrasts the lion with the wolf who harries the dying. Again, we are put in mind of Yvain's early conduct. Similarly, Claudian uses the traditional self-control and *magnanimitas* of the lion to sing the praises of the emperor Stilicho: 'All who oppose you, you overthrow, but you do not deign to touch them when overthrown, like a lion who lusts to rend in pieces the fierce bull, but passes by the cowering prey' (see *7*, p.5). Note how Chrétien portrays the giant Harpin: 'bret et crie *come tors*; / que mout l'a li lions grevé' (ll.4228-29). The references to the *magnanimitas* of the lion were naturally reinforced, in their application to rulers, by a celebrated passage from the *Aeneid* VI, 851-53 — the words of Anchises: 'Remember, O Roman, to rule the nations with your sway — these shall be your arts — to crown peace with law, to spare the humbled, and to tame in war the proud [*parcere subiectis et debellere superbos*]' (see *10*, p.567). The final phrase was rapidly appropriated by religious writers to elaborate the Christian ideal of the *rex*, not only *justus*, but *pius*. Thus Augustine in the preface to *The City of God*:

Well do I know the powers needed to persuade the proud how great is the virtue of humility, that lofty quality by which our city is raised above all earthly heights that are rocked by ever-streaming time, not raised by the devices of human arrogance but by the endowment of grace divine. For the King and Founder of this City, which is the subject of my discourse, has revealed in the scripture of his people a statement of divine law, which I quote: 'God resists the proud but gives grace to the humble' [*James* 4,6]. Indeed, it is this distinction, which belongs to God, that the inflated fancy of a proud spirit assumes when it chooses to be praised in the following terms: 'To spare the fallen and subdue the proud' [*parcere subiectis et debellare superbos*]

(see *4*, pp.11-13).

This passage is referred to by Alcuin in a letter of 799 A.D. addressed to Charlemagne, praising the virtue of mercy: 'We read that one of the ancient poets, singing the praises of the Roman emperors, if I remember correctly, and explaining how they should conduct themselves, said '*Parcere subiectis et debellare superbos*', a verse which the blessed Augustine commended in *The City of God*'. So popular did the Virgilian motto become that it even entered the *artes dictandi* as a formula to be used when writing to emperors and various dignitaries!

What we have, therefore, in the period leading up to the age which produced *Yvain*, is the coalescence of the Virgilian idea with a traditional property of the lion, an amalgam so potent that it crystallized in a tag which is found in countless twelfth-century productions. The tag first appears in the pseudo-Ovidian *De mirabilibus mundi* (On the Marvels of the World), a work of 126 leonine hexameters which seem to have been intended as rubrics for book illustrations or, possibly, wall paintings, and whose author seems to have been Thierry, abbot of Saint-Trond from 1099-1107. The 70th rubric runs 'The anger of the noble lion may spare the defeated: do likewise, whoever governs here on earth' (*Parcere prostratis scit nobilis ira leonis; / Tu quoque fac simile quisquis dominaris in orbes*). It is subsequently found in a number of twelfth-century works (see

Hunt, *57*, p.97), the first hexameter being given a special moral *adaptatio* in Alexander Nequam's *De naturis rerum*. Even if the animal is famished, says Nequam, and a man should prostrate himself at its feet, the lion spares him, for its 'royal nobility' (*regia nobilitas*) dispenses mercy to the suppliant, as Our Lord resisted the proud and spared the humble. Similarly, in his *De laudibus divinae sapientiae* (In Praise of the Divine Wisdom) Nequam repeats the idea in a couplet that the lion is pleased to spare the suppliant and resist those puffed up with pride and this forms the title to its 'clara nobilitas'. The image of the lion sprang readily to the minds of poets who were concerned with the favour of a patron. In his 'Confessions' the Archpoet seeks the mercy of the Archbishop of Cologne by invoking the lion 'which forgets its anger before the humble and spares them'. Also in the twelfth century, the troubadour Bertran de Born, in a plea for clemency to Richard Cœur de Lion (in 1194), says 'The lion's custom appeals to me, who is not cruel to a creature once overcome, but who is proud in the face of pride' (see Press, *8*, p.167).

It will be recalled that Chrétien prefaces his romance with a programmatic *sententia*, 'Qu'ancor vaut miauz, ce m'est vis, / Uns cortois morz qu'uns vilains vis' (ll.31-32). He then depicts Yvain, open to criticism on more than one count, savaging and slaying a mortally wounded *cortois*, Esclados. The moral *vilainie* of the hero is then converted through a symbolic death (lament at the fountain followed by madness) to a new courtly identity, that of the Knight of the Lion, who acquires the attributes of the *rex justus et pius* and finally retakes possession of his lands. It is certain that with his lion Yvain humbles the proud and succours the meek and needy. The tradition concerning the lion which we traced above surely explains its choice and significance in the romance. Perhaps Chrétien playfully provided a clue by making his opening *sententia* an inversion of Ecclesiastes IX,4: 'A living dog is better than a dead lion'.

There is a striking congruence between the conception of the lion outlined above and the text of *Yvain*. Yet, we must begin by acknowledging that the lion is a symbolic adjunct which neither initiates nor terminates the hero's chivalric exploits. The defence of the Dame de Noroison is really undertaken through divine aid (cf. the refs. at ll.2934, 2942, 2948, 3013) or, rather, through what appears as a courtly burlesque of divine healing (cf. Mark 16,1ff.) in which a magic ointment prepared by Morgan is used. The principal purpose of the episode seems to be to establish the principle of reciprocity and gratitude. Thus, the hero 'qui grant *mestier* eüst / d'aïe' (ll.3046-47) says to one of the maidens sent by his unknown benefactress 'Dameisele! or me dites donc, / se vos avez *mestier* de moi?' (ll.3078-79). In gratitude for his cure Yvain defends the castle against the invading Count Alier and fires the otherwise pusillanimous knights with courage (ll.3171-83, 3205-11). Against the manifest wickedness of his opponents Yvain fights like a famished lion (ll.3202-04)!

The comparison of the hero with Roland (ll.3235-37), the reflection that his love would be highly prized (ll.3243-44), and the metaphors of light (ll.3245-49), recalling the 'sun of chivalry' Gawain, establish at once Yvain's exemplariness. Only recently cast off for dereliction of his conjugal and defensive duties, he is now seen as the ideal partner for the Dame de Noroison and as a knight who may fittingly have 'la terre an sa justise' (l.3254). He is 'li cortois, li preuz, li buens / mes sire Yvains' (ll.3192-93). As if to complete this picture of a reformed Yvain, Chrétien depicts the capture of Alier as the antithesis of the slaughter of Esclados: the enemy is spared, restitution is made, pledges are handed over (there is even a textual parallel in ll.511f. and 3261f.). The implication of this remarkable restoration to exemplariness is that Yvain is 'cured', both physically and morally. The slate is clean. The introduction of the lion, therefore, serves the *elaboration* of the chivalric ideal, pursued, not in respect of a personal relationship, but as a public demonstration in which the hero is cast, not in the role of lover, but of ruler — *justus et pius*.

The first concept which is associated with the introduction of the lion is, appropriately, *pitié*, for it is compassion which leads Yvain to assist the lion without consideration of self-interest (ll.3373-75). The rescue of the lion is the only exploit in which we are given a clear indication of the hero's reaction to his experience (see evidence of his thoughts at ll.3354ff., 3362ff.,

3389f.). After the lion's display of gratitude to Yvain we are informed: 'Si li plest mout ceste avanture' (l.3407, cf. l.1038). The lion's role is henceforward to 'serve and protect' (l.3415) its master and it is on account of such 'grant amor' (l.3455) that Yvain accepts its companionship. Following the demonstration of the beast's humility (ll.3401, 3404) in a gesture of quasi-feudal homage, the hunting scene illustrates its power. As a sustainer of life the fearless beast replaces the timorous charity of the hermit (cf. ll.2861-64). We await, however, the first illustration of the lion's part as a symbol of morally discriminating force, guided by its master and inspired by the notion of reciprocity.

It is all the more surprising, therefore, to arrive at the next episode and discover that it involves a suicide attempt by the lion! And yet, this is perhaps best interpreted as an extreme demonstration of reciprocity. Yvain had felt *pitié* for the lion in distress and now the lion reveals an almost sublime degree of compassion with the suffering of its master, without whom it is nothing. The lion seeks no independence of its master (see ll.3430f.): henceforth they are inseparable. But Chrétien perfectly understands the force of 'our sincerest laughter with some pain is fraught'. Humour and the sublime are near neighbours. The scene does not lack gentle comedy. In the last episode involving the lion Chrétien will again introduce a note of comedy, by recording the detail of the excited beast momentarily getting stuck under the gate as it seeks to break out of its enclosure to assist its master (ll.5612f.)! The 'fausse morte' episode, based on illusion, not deceit, symbolizes the annihilation of the 'old' Yvain. The hero entreats Lunete to preserve his anonymity (ll.3728-31, 4639-42) henceforward.

The first of the three adventures in which the lion actively participates begins with an indication of the fear which the animal is capable of inspiring in others (ll.3789-93). The solidarity of master and beast is affirmed in Yvain's words 'autretant l'aim come mon cors' (l.3798). The hero himself displays a remarkable degree of empathy in the face of the suffering of Gawain's relatives (ll.3846-50, 3903-04), a quality already commended through the lion's suicide attempt, and it is once more *pitié* (ll.3942, 4070, 4075 [var.]) which engages his support for the oppressed. The references to God (ll.3877, 4138, 4157, 4177) suggest, as in later episodes, a Providential framework within which the hero is moved to act. The present adventure clearly illustrates humility disarming and overcoming pride. Yvain will not accept the obeisance of the family he seeks to assist: 'Des m'an deffande, / qu'*orguiauz* an moi tant ne s'estande, / que a mon pié venir les les' (ll.3983-85). The giant Harpin is described as 'cil jaianz, qui la fors *s'orguelle*' (l.4137), 'qui an sa force se fioit, / tant que armer ne se deignoit' (ll.4209-10). Although the inhabitants of the castle still stand in awe of the lion (ll.4024-29), they recognize in it a sign of its master's nobility as it 'aussi doucement se gist / lez lui, come uns aigniaus feïst' (ll.4011-12). We may see in it a symbol of both the *corteisie* and *proesce* which the narrator commends in the hero (ll.4022-23) and which provide the distinctive combination of strength and humility, aggression and submission, which, as we have seen, a notable tradition associated with the lion. It is the *ira* (*ire*, l.4221), the 'anger of the noble lion', which secures the crucial intervention, so permitting Yvain's recovery and enabling him personally to deal the fatal blows to the giant, who, with his pride, is never *prostratus* and consequently is not shown mercy. Harpin is the epitome of *vilainie*, associated with pride, whilst Yvain represents *corteisie*, linked with *pitié*. How far the new chivalric ideal receives the sanction of God and Justice is left to the next adventure, but the hero already takes the name 'Chevalier au lion' and thereby commits himself to the virtues symbolized by the lion.

In the next adventure Yvain returns to the fountain to rescue Lunete. It is significant that he earlier insists on punctuality (ll.3993ff.) and refuses to make a promise which he cannot guarantee to keep (ll.3999f.), envisaging madness as the unavoidable consequence, should unpunctuality occur (ll.4080-82). The central, motivating power of *pitié* is again made clear (l.4357), together with an unequivocal confidence in the support of God and Justice (ll.4332f., 4443-48), which are associated as 'conpaignons' with the hero's lion (ll.4335-36). In this episode Yvain gives no assurance that the beast will not intervene, contenting himself and his opponents with ensuring its withdrawal at the outset of the battle. It is clearly not demoted to the status of non-combatant, however, and in the event there is an obviously significant coincidence of the lion's intervention with the prayers of the ladies at court (ll.4509-21), a moment emphasized by the narrator's observation concerning the combatants, 'or sont el chanp tot per a per' (l.4533). Nevertheless, Yvain seeks to drive away the lion, 'mes li lions sanz dote set, / que ses sire mie ne het / s'aïe, einçois l'an aimme plus' (ll.4543-45). For the first time the lion is injured and Yvain is spurred to avenge it (l.4552f.), yet the combat ends in a way that is entirely consonant with the lion's incorporation of strength and humility. The seneschal's brothers at last offer no resistance to Yvain, but 'an sa merci se randent / por l'aïe, que li a feite / li lions, qui mout se desheite' (ll.4556-58). Here the opponents are *prostrati* and are shown mercy. It is Laudine's court which operates the *lex talionis*, the principle of an eye for an eye, and the narrator's approval is in all probability a literary borrowing from Ovid (*Ars amatoria* I, 653ff.). The hero, who was given aid when the lion understood 'que mestiers li est' (l.4511), now reciprocates by bearing the wounded beast on his shield (ll.4652ff.). As the lion showed compassion at the hero's self-inflicted wound at the fountain, so now Yvain is heedless of his own pain and thinks only of his companion (ll.4564f.). His identity as the 'Chevalier au lion' is once more affirmed (ll.4613f.), this time in conjunction with a striking modesty formula: 'Dame! par ce savoir poez, / que ne sui gueires renomez' (ll.4619f.). This assertion before Laudine is ironically belied by the younger sister's search (ll.4816-20) in the inheritance dispute, where the messenger tells the hero 'Li granz renons de vostre pris / M'a mout fet aprés vos lasser' (ll.5060-61; cf. l.5075).

At Pesme Avanture, the third adventure in which the lion plays an important role, the animal displays its anger the moment it sees the opponents ('netuns') and their arms (ll.5526ff.). It beats the ground with its tail, a sure sign of its anger according to the bestiaries (*Yvain*, ll.5532-35). There is a clear gradation in Yvain's responses to the assistance rendered by the lion, and he now, in the most difficult of all his exploits, openly affirms his desire for its aid (ll.5547ff.). The opponents ludicrously declare that this is unfair, for 'Dui seriiez contre nos deus' (l.5560). It is, of course, the manifest inequality of the combatants in three of the adventures which justifies on the simplest level the lion's intervention. It is now that the part played by the lion is explicitly characterized as reciprocation of a service already rendered:

> Ore a le cuer dolant et troble
> Li lions, qui est an la chanbre
> Que de la grant bonté li manbre,
> Que cil li fist par sa franchise,
> Qui ja avroit de son servise
> Et de s'aïe grant mestier.
> Ja li randroit au grant sestier
> Et au grant mui ceste bonté,
> Ja n'i avroit rien mesconté,
> S'il pooit issir de leanz.
>
> (ll.5594-603)

Again, mercy and ferocity are proportional according to the conduct of the opponents. He who is *prostratus* is always spared. In this instance it is the surviving *netun*:

> 'Ostez vostre lion, biaus sire!
> Se vos plest, que plus ne m'adoist!
> Que des or mes feire vos loist
> De moi tot, quanque buen vos iert.
> Et qui merci prie et requiert,
> N'i doit faillir, quant il la rueve,
> Se home sanz pitié ne trueve.
> Et je ne me deffandrai plus
> Ne ja ne me leverai sus
> De ci por ce, que merci aie,
> Si me met an vostre menaie.'
>
> (ll.5676-86)

Having extracted a formal acknowledgement from his opponent that he is *recreant*, Yvain tells him: 'Donc n'as tu mes garde de moi, / et mes lions te rasseüre' (ll.5692-93).

The direct participation of the lion in its master's adventures, graded so that in each case it is both later and fiercer, is now at an end, and with it, we might say, the *societas leonina* (in which the hero receives his companion's share) of the second half of the romance. The *nobilis ira leonis* is a potent reminder throughout of the distinctive combination of force and service and brings into being the pseudonym 'Chevalier au lion', which alone permits the stratagem by which Laudine is finally rewon, as well as indicating a new chivalric ideal which contrasts with the hero's self-centred pursuit of *gloire* in the first part of the romance.

6. Sic et Non

Do Yvain and Gawain, locked in arduous combat, really love each other? asks the narrator (l.6001) — '«Oïl» vos respong et «nenil»' (l.6002). Does Yvain wish his opponent harm? — 'Oïl, et il lui autressi' (l.6072). And would Gawain harm his friend? — 'Nenil ... li uns ne voldroit avoir fet / A l'autre ne honte ne let' (ll.6076-78). The dialectical nature of the answers — 'Yes and No' (cf. ll.1454-60) — inevitably brings to mind the title of Abelard's famous treatise *Sic et Non*, which appeared in 1121 and gave notoriety to the fast developing discipline of dialectic in the schools (see Hunt, *52*). In his treatise Abelard juxtaposed seemingly contradictory passages from both canon law and Scripture and suggested in an introduction how such 'apparent' contradictions or discrepancies might be reconciled. With comparable intellectual virtuosity Chrétien's narrator shows how Amor and Haïne coexist in the combatants Yvain and Gawain, how there can be a single meeting place for 'deus choses, qui sont contreires' (l.6026), and how the paradox of a knight both loving and hating his opponent can be made to yield nuances of meaning which transcend what appears to be a contradiction. This is a very important discovery which needs to be pondered when we attend to the conclusion of the romance where there seems to be an uncomfortable discrepancy between Laudine's indignant complaint to Lunete 'me feras amer *maugré mien*' (l.6763) and the narrator's assurance that Yvain is 'amez et chier tenuz / de sa dame' (ll.6804-05).

All the conventional expectations of the troubadour lyrics are here undercut. Laudine does not display mercy (*merce*), never appearing to share in the hero's acquisition of *pitié*; she is not moved by the suppliant's fair words (the decision is taken at l.6776, before Yvain says a thing); she does not conform to the notion of reciprocity, praised by Bernart de Ventadorn and illustrated in the relationships of Yvain and Gawain, Yvain and

Lunete, and Yvain and the lion. Should we go so far as Bernart does when he argues in several lyrics that his lady is guilty of the selfsame faults that she imputes to him? For example, does Laudine understand any better than Yvain how lovers behave (ll.2760ff.)? If Yvain took away the lady's heart (ll.2725ff.), has she not removed also his joy?

> 'Dame! vos an portez la clef,
> Et la serre et l'escrin avez,
> Ou ma joie est, si nel savez.'
>
> (ll.4632-34)

Is the ending an ironic reaffirmation of the changeable nature of women, in particular their perversity? In treating of the love of Troïlus and Briseïda the author of the *Roman de Troie* has an excursus on women in which he declares,

> A femme dure dueus petit:
> A l'un ueil plore, a l'autre rit.
> Mout muënt tost li lor corage.
> Assez est fole la plus sage:
> Quant qu'ele a en set anz amé
> A ele en treis jorz oblié.
>
> (*1*, ll.13441-46)

Laudine has been widowed after seven years of marriage (ll.2088-89), but her 'recovery' so soon after the funeral, where she attracts the longing of the hero, reminds us of Ovid's cynical comment,

> Often a husband is sought for at a husband's funeral; it is becoming to go with dishevelled hair, and to mourn without restraint. (*Ars amatoria* III, 431-32; *5*, p.149)

The narrator made it clear that Laudine was glad of the pressure brought by her barons, so that she might do as she desired whilst retaining her public dignity (ll.2137-49). Does not Lunete's final stratagem with the oath on the relics serve the same purpose?

Laudine is once again enabled to feign reluctance as a face-saving measure. Once more we recall Ovid:

> You may use force: women like you to use it; they often wish to give unwillingly what they like to give. She whom a sudden assault has taken by storm is pleased, and counts the audacity as a compliment.
>
> (*Ars amatoria* I, 673-76; 5, p.59)

Is the function of the storm at the fountain, then, to mask the 'folor' of women (cf. ll.1640ff.) by supplying the motif of coercion? Are we not tempted to provide a dialectical answer 'oïl et nenil' by arguing that Laudine does love Yvain, but does not wish to be seen to 'change' to loving him so quickly? The contrived ambiguity of the lovers' reunion forces us to probe beyond the surface configurations of plot and posture. Like so much of *Yvain*, it is designed to produce *debate*! Is the injunction 'Pardonez li [= Yvain] vostre ire' (l.6756) fulfilled by Laudine's apparently grudging recognition of her legal obligation?

The sort of debate in which Chrétien invites his audience to engage is itself mirrored in a succession of debates within the romance: Lunete arguing with Laudine about the relative merits of the combatants (viz. Yvain and Esclados) at the fountain (ll.1693-1711); Laudine debating with herself about the guilt or innocence of the man who slew her husband (ll.1753-56); Lunete and Yvain discussing at the chapel which of them is the more wretched (ll.3573-616); the narrator's dialectical analysis of the roles of Amor and Haïne in the combat of Yvain and Gawain (ll.5998ff.). These debates find their models in both the *partimens* of troubadour poetry (Laudine's inner debate is called *tançon* in l.1735, cf. Provençal *tenso*) and in the dialectic of the schools and display the same formal virtuosity and theoretical subtlety which characterize the *casuistry* of twelfth-century romance (see Gruber, *42*). The verb *prover* is used four times in the sense of 'to demonstrate logically' (ll.1611, 1657, 1704, 1773). There are clear echoes of syllogistic reasoning (ll.998-1000), including the enthymeme (syllogism with one premise unexpressed, see, for example, ll.3542-47), and of forensic terminology (ll.1754ff., 1992ff.). Laudine twice expresses distrust of verbal and semantic virtuosity (ll.1700-01, 6761). Chrétien has carried over from his previous romance, *Cligés*, much of the courtly delight in logic chopping and rhetorical subtlety.

It is important to give full recognition to the dialectical nature of the rhetoric of *Yvain* because it is the constant exploitation of *contrasts* which gives this work its unmistakably dramatic character. In addition, these contrasts reinforce what has been called 'the fundamentally adversative rhythm underlying *Le Chevalier au Lion (Yvain)*' (see Grimbert, *41*, p.27), a description suggested by the realization that, in Roques's edition of the romance, 250 out of the 6806 lines begin with *mes* ('but'). Since Chrétien's artistry in *Yvain* has been well illustrated by Frappier (see *35*, pp.219-72), who has examined in particular detail the structure of the couplet (see *33*, pp.247ff.), and Chrétien's syntax has been studied by Biller (see *15*), we shall concentrate here on rhetoric and dialectic, showing how they contribute to the dramatic verve of the romance and to the formulation of critical questions.

We have already seen how the introduction to *Yvain* is constructed on a series of contrasts and reversals, culminating in the striking antithesis of the *vilains vis* and the *cortois morz* (ll.31-32). The repetition of the fountain adventure, too, establishes a crucial ethical contrast between the unknowing Calogrenant and the disingenuous Yvain, who is fully aware of the consequences of pouring water on the stone and provoking the legal complaint of the offended fountain knight. The most general name for the rhetorical figure of opposition or antithesis is *contentio*. Here are a few examples:

> Mes *l'amors* devandra *haïne* (l.2564)
>
> Se vos *mantez*, je *dirai voir* (l.2569)
>
> Et con plus *liee* l'avoit feite,
> Plus li *poise* et plus li *desheite* (ll.3327-28)

Qui a *duel* ai *joie* changiee (l.3553)

Tes *diaus* est *joie*, tes *maus biens* (l.3576)

The figure of *contentio* is frequently given emphasis by being used at the rhyme: *proesce — peresce* (ll.79-80); *joianz — dolanz* (ll.677-78); *sagemant — folemant* (ll.933-34); *acoardie — hardie* (ll.1227-28); *fiel — miel* (ll.1401-02); *anemis — amis* (ll.1459-60); *liee — iriee* (ll.1489-90); *vilenie — corteisie* (ll.2213-14); *perdu — randu* (ll.2933-34); *ocis — vis* (ll.3747- 48). Sometimes the contrast is made by breaking the rhyme: *vuidier — plains* (ll.88-89). Often, of course, the antithesis provides the formulation of a paradox:

Qu'ancor vaut miauz, ce m'est avis,
Uns *cortois morz* qu'uns *vilains vis* (ll.31-32)

S'*aimme* la rien, qui plus le *het* (l.1361)

Ançois *amerai m'anemie* (l.1450)

Et plus est buens a essaiier
Uns *petiz* biens, quant il *delaie*,
Qu'uns *granz*, que l'an *adés essaie* (ll.2516-18)

Tes *diaus* est *joie*, tes *maus biens* (l.3576)

The most fundamental opposition of the romance remains, of course, that of the terms *vilain* and *cortois*. But the opposition is not simple and we have to discover the implications of the terms as the romance progresses. The word *vilain* is used to describe Kay (l.90), the herdsman (ll.288, 294 etc.), the crowd at Pesme Avanture (l.5119), the battle with the *netuns* (l.5607) and the position of Laudine without a defender of the fountain (l.6570). That is to say, the word is used in situations where the hero is expected to supply a remedy. In the first half of the work, however, the word is used, with deliberate irony, in its social rather than moral sense to suggest a paradoxical contrast. The herdsman is outwardly a *vilain*, but turns out to be an admirable figure in his conduct. Conversely, Yvain's nobility of birth is remarked on by Laudine with the words 'cist n'est mie vilains' (l.1816), but morally his conduct overturns expectations. In the first half of the work *cortois/cortoisie* may be co-ordinated with such obviously desirable qualities as *proesce, san, bon' eire* or adjectives such as *sage*. Yet, at the end of *Yvain*, *cortois* and *cortoisemant* are employed to characterize Lunete and her deception of Laudine (ll.6630, 6635).

Once oppositions have been grasped, their substance must be carefully attended to. We need to give full value to the notion 'de cuer antandre' and reflect carefully on the oppositions of the text such as presence — absence, love — hate, beauty — sorrow, appearance — reality. We are, as it were, on a semantic quest, a quest which turns back on itself. *Yvain* is a sort of *roman à rebours*: the hero's quest for the fountain leads him away from true chivalry and the way forward lies in *return* to the fountain — at first through *avanture* (l.3490), a turning point in his career, and finally through an effort of the will inspired by love. The inversion of motifs is significant — he cannot bear being parted from Laudine (ll.6513ff.) and this time he will depart 'toz seus de cort' (l.6518) in a very different spirit from that of his solitary departure (ll.679, 693, 725) from Arthur's court at the beginning of the romance.

Alongside subtle cross references (see, for example, the pair *enor — honte* in ll.60 and 721), Chrétien exploits a variety of word repetitions. When a single word is inflected through several forms, the figure is known as *traductio*: *veoir, veüe, voi* (ll.1213ff.); *coarz, coardise, coarde, acoardie* (ll.1222ff.); *fantosmes, anfantosmee* (ll.1220ff.); *amer, amerai, aim, amoit* (ll.1450ff.); *lerre, larron* (ll.2724ff.); *anbler, anble, anblent* (ll.2728ff.). This form of expressive repetition can be refined by the use of *annominatio* (paronomasia), in which the repeated words share an etymologically or phonetically identical radical, thus: *cort* (ll.4257-59); *oste, ostel, oster, ost* (ll.1379ff.); *fin* (noun), *fin* (adj.), *fine* (adj.), *fine* (verb) (ll.6811-13). A particularly striking example of extended *annominatio* is found in the account of the young maiden's quest for Yvain to secure his services for the younger sister of Noire Espine:

> Tant que vint a la *nuit* oscure,
> Si li *enuia* mout la *nuiz*.
> Et de ce dobla li *enuiz*
> ...
> Et la *nuiz* et li bois li font
> Grant *enui*, mes plus li *enuie*,
> Que li bois ne la *nuiz*, la pluie.
>   (ll.4838-40/4844-46)

The figures of *traductio* and *annominatio* may be combined, as in 'enuieus enuiier et nuire' (l.118).

The mere classification of rhetorical figures is, of course, arid, and what needs to be appreciated is the dramatic variety which they may impart to the narrative, especially through the provision of contrasts. Thus we find the striking figure of *correctio*, through which a statement is immediately modified: 'Et donc sui je ses anemis? / Nenil certes, mes ses amis' (ll.1459f.), 'Ore ai je manti leidemant' (l.6081). Another emphatic figure involving contrast is litotes (a form of understatement based on denial of the opposite):

> Don je ne me ting mie a sage (l.434)
>
> Qu'ele n'estoit mie legiere (l.534)
>
> Qui sa dolur mie ne cele (l.1410)
>
> N'estoient ne fausses ne faintes (l.4388)
>
> Si n'avez mie fet savoir (l.5222)

Repetition of words in specific positions involves the use of anaphora (*repetitio*) and anadiplosis. Anaphora consists in the repetition of a word at the beginning of successive clauses, as in the following example:

> *S'il viaut* armes, an li atorne,
> *S'il viaut* cheval, an li sejorne
>   (ll.3139-40)

Other examples are 'An tel ...' (ll.2025-31), 'Veez ...' (ll.3212-14, 3216-17), 'Come ...' (ll.3218-19), 'Li anemi ...' (ll.6048-49). Anadiplosis involves the repetition of the end of one phrase at the beginning of the text. It is particularly suited to dialogue of the exploratory and analytical kind which we find in *Yvain* and is well illustrated in the exchange of Yvain and Laudine in ll.2015-24 and in the narrator's rhetorical question in ll.1278f.: 'Si li eüst costé mil mars. / Mil mars? ...' A related figure is chiasmus in which a sequence of words is then inverted in a kind of mirror image:

> An mon *cors* por qu'areste l'*ame*?
> Que fet *ame* an si dolant *cors*? (ll.3536-37)

> Mout *se doit* bien *haïr* de mort.
> *Haïr* et ocirre *se doit*. (ll.3544-45)

The lexical richness of Old French encouraged the use of figures involving synonymy. This is often observed in the syntactic feature of polysyndeton, that is, the employment of frequent connective particles (as opposed to asyndeton — no connectives):

> prandre et anclorre et retenir (l.164)

> Ele fu longue et gresle et droite (l.229)

> Or te pri et quier et demant (l.364)

> Tres sage et veziiee et cointe (l.2417)

Even more characteristic of Old French narrative poetry is the use of binomial expressions, often known as synonymic pairs, which seem in origin to be part of a popular expressivity which was also exploited in Latin poetry and was facilitated by the requirements of the Old French octosyllabic line. A striking concentration is found in the following lines:

> Que pitiez l'an *semont et prie*,
> Qu'il face *secors et aïe*

A la beste *jantil et franche*.

(ll.3373-75)

The technique is widespread throughout Old French (see Diekamp, *28*) and may be combined with alliteration, anaphora (each synonym preceded by the same word), and *annominatio* (synonyms etymologically related) (see Nordahl, *66*). Thus, alliteration is present in:

> Et angoisseus et antrepris (l.3641)
>
> Desheitiee et desconfortee (l.5818)
>
> Et desconfite et desjuglee (l.6060)
>
> La mescheance et li meschiés (l.6328)

Anaphora is exemplified in:

> Et tel *fierté* et tel *orguel* (l.283)
>
> Sanz grant *enui* et sanz *pesance* (l.405)
>
> Sanz rien *grever* et sanz rien *nuire* (l.1918)
>
> Par son *mesfet* et par son *tort* (l.3543)

There is also the case of hyperbaton (displacement of grammatical word order):

> *Comander* vos vuel et *priier* (l.136)

Besides attention to the disposition of words there is also in Chrétien a playful attitude to etymology, which underlies, for example, the comparison of Lunete to the moon (ll.2395-414), whilst a more learned one applies to the juxtaposition of *prosnes* (choir-screen) and *ramposnes* (two MSS have the earlier form *ramprosnes*), which are etymologically related (ll.629-30).

These examples of the verbal rhetoric of *Yvain* will suffice to indicate the liveliness of Chrétien's style. But there are other important aspects of the dramatic qualities of *Yvain* which remain to be touched on. A high proportion of the text, approximately 46 per cent, is taken up by direct speech (nearly 3200 lines), which is particularly prominent in the first part of the romance, up to the leave-taking (ll.1-2638), where it occupies as much as 55 per cent of the text. Monologues are rare (the most striking is Yvain's at ll.1428-1506), whilst dialogues are highly characteristic of Chrétien's dramatic style — striking, extended examples occur at ll.978-1085, 1428-1506, 1598-1726, 1795-1877, 1959-2048, 3570-769, 3835-954, 5247-346. In particular, the wooing of Laudine displays features of contemporary dramatic productions in Latin, the so-called 'elegiac comedies', especially the *Pamphilus* and *De nuntio sagaci* (see Hunt, *53*) which were products of the transition from the would-be poet's imitation of school authors in Latin to his writing a vernacular narrative for a lay patron.

The role of the narrator in *Yvain* also merits attention, narratorial observations occupying some 500 lines of the work. The narrator's presence is marked by about 20 occurrences of the first person pronoun *je/me/moi* and *nos*, and by even more instances of first person verbs without pronouns (e.g. ll.1509, 1950: there are over 30 examples). In addition, there are phrases like 'au mien esciant' (l.2366) and 'ma parole' (l.2394). The audience is evoked on about 30 occasions in the following ways: use of second person plural pronoun *vos* (ll.1749, 1950, 2161 etc.); second person plural interrogatory or imperative (ll.2399, 3392 etc.); second person plural verb with personal pronoun (ll.777, 3509 etc.). These references all assist in promoting the atmosphere of debate, encouraging the audience to interpret what it hears. There are requests for attention (ll.1749, 3392, 5397ff.), assurances of veracity (ll.777, 1950, 6067 etc.), hyperbolic emphases (ll.2161, 3508, 5389, 6460), expressions of ironic distance (ll.2393, 2624, 2629) and questions (ll.2399, 6013, 6015 etc.). There is a notable lightness of touch in the narrator's dealings with his audience. Whether directed explicitly to his audience or not, his comments are local, often ironic, dramatic (generating suspense), and playful, signs of an *esprit dégagé* which is content to leave to the listener the task of making up his mind about the interpretation of events. *Yvain* is the least didactic of Chrétien's romances.

Surprisingly little use is made of rhetorical questions (ll.1594ff., 2629ff., 5354), but there is considerable use of hyperbole (e.g. ll.1146-49, 1174-76, 2051f., 2403ff., 3508-10, 4245-47, 4841f., 5375ff.). The discreet nature of the narrator's presence is confirmed by his not infrequent attempts to efface himself through modesty formulae such as the inexpressibility topos (ll.787-90, 2159-63, 2388-92, 6535-37), feigned ignorance (ll.4700, 5356, 5366, 5407, 5872), brevity formulae (ll.2393f., 2624ff., 2918f., 5389ff., 5836ff.). Source references are strikingly few (ll.2685, 6814-18, cf. 2151-53), assertions of truth are discreet (ll.2366f., 4329f., 6076, 6535), the use of *exclamatio* sparing (ll.2037, 5424f., 6021, 6024), apostrophe (e.g. to Love, l.6045) uncommon, excessive hyperbole rare (ll.5375ff., 5780ff.). The heavy hand of didacticism is carefully avoided. The use of the excursus is confined almost wholly to debating points about love (ll.1386-1405, 1640-44, 5385-96). Sententious commentary is courtly rather than moralistic (ll.785-90, 1940-42, 2146f. [= Ovid, *Ars amatoria* II,731], ll.2459-65, 2644ff., 3173-80, 4280-81). Expressions of opinion are usually modest and cautious — *ce cuit* (ll.2661f., 3009), *ce me sanble* (ll.3157, 3486), *n'est (pas) mervoille* (ll.1947, 6213) — and it is only in the celebrated commentary on the combat of Yvain and Gawain that the narrator is moved to explicit engagement with his audience (cf. ll.2399ff.). The use of *praesumptio* (prolepsis), that is, anticipation, reflects a concern for the action of the story and the tension it may generate, rather than for directing the audience's interpretation (see ll.772-76, 1375f., 1945, 2661-71, 3413ff., 3782f. [see 3891ff.], 5424f., 5860f., 6226ff.). There are few retrogressive references (ll.896ff., 1284f., 2421f., 2471f., 5011f.).

Yvain is a work which is free from all forms of excess and which is allusive and critical, rather than affirmative and explicit. There is a good deal less description than in Chrétien's *Erec* and the literary portraits (e.g. the herdsman, ll.288ff., Laudine, ll.1462ff.) are the more memorable for being few in number (cf. Colby, *23*). The pace of the narrative is swift and its texture dramatic. The language is sobre, there being few rare words, but there are colourful similes drawn from the world of nature (ll.814, 882-84, 3195, 3524f. etc., see Ziltener, *91*) and from literary sources (e.g. Ovid in ll.1777-80, 2146f., 2519-23, 4348-51) (for a survey of similes in Old French literature see Vogel, *87*). It is difficult to believe that the work propounds a thesis or incorporates a spiritual 'sen'. Attempts to provide an allegorized interpretation of the work unfailingly call to mind Horace Walpole's description of the novels of Richardson, 'romances as they would be spiritualized by a Methodist preacher' (see, as a recent example of the genre, Heffernan, *47*).

In the final analysis the conduct of both Yvain and Laudine remains in part enigmatic. The love theme seems best approached through the troubadour lyrics which are really part of a great debate on the pros and cons of loving an imperious lady (*dompna*). The poetry of Bernart de Ventadorn will, once again, serve to clarify the dialectic of the hero's dilemma. In one poem Bernart laments,

> Through my own fault I find myself no longer her close friend, for I failed to return to her on account of a folly [*foudat*] which keeps me back. I experience such shame at having been away so long, that I dare not approach her unless I obtain some reassurance from her first.
>
> (*3*, 15, 17-24)

Is it such 'reassurance' that Yvain may be seeking when, incognito, he speaks to his lady at the fountain after he has freed Lunete? If so, he is apparently not satisfied by the assurance he receives. In the same poem, Bernart depicts the determination of the lover who, having read (in Ovid, *Ars amatoria* I,475f. and *Ex Ponto* 4,10,5!) that slowly the drop of water hollows out the stone, will persevere until his lady is moved by pity for his plight (see *Yvain*, ll.4588ff.). But, as other poems remind us, excessive waiting is destructive of love. Between these poles the lover languishes almost to death and the despair finally experienced by Yvain (ll.6511ff.) is comparable with that depicted in Bernart's *Amors, enquera.us preyara* (*3*, 12, 45-55). Having passed through all these stages, Yvain is left with only one way of resolving the situation and that is to force a confrontation with Laudine.

If Yvain is seen to enact the different possibilities in the conduct of the courtly lover and to illustrate various aspects of his dilemma, it still remains unclear how relevant all this is to the hero's remarkable and impressive chivalric career after he has been cast off by Laudine. A century ago E. Philipot wrote:

> Quel est le motif précis qui pousse Yvain à errer sans fin, après qu'il a entendu son arrêt? Est-ce une expiation qu'il s'impose à lui-même? Son arrière-pensée est-elle d'acquérir tant de gloire que sa dame éblouie ne puisse faire autre chose que de rendre son amour à un chevalier si brave; veut-il la reconquérir par l'admiration, en sorte qu'après avoir rappelé le Cid dans sa première partie, le Chevalier au lion ferait songer à Polyeucte dans la seconde? Tout cela n'est pas nettement indiqué et l'art de Chrétien dans la composition, malgré de grands progrès sur l'épopée ancienne, est encore loin d'être sûr. (*70*, pp.463-64)

Mais nous avons changé tout cela. Chrétien seems, one hundred years later, to be a poet of magisterial control and subtlety. The accepted view is that his romances deal with the careful co-ordination of love and chivalry in perfect knighthood or the coalescence of courtly love and conjugal affection in perfect marriage. For our part, we dissent from this interpretation and from the two assumptions which underly the most recent full-length study of Chrétien (see Topsfield, *85*), namely, that Chrétien's *œuvre* is a unitary creation, homogeneous, interlocking and consistent; and that from this can be derived a serious, essentially moral (or even moralistic) view of the world, which invites the use of labels such as Christian humanism. Against this view of moral *engagement* we should argue that Chrétien is a dialectician who juxtaposes rather than harmonizes, who is committed to no single belief, and who *experiments* in each of his romances with various combinations of contemporary debating points. The difficulties set forth by Philipot are still with us, as can be seen from their reflection in the following statement by Faith Lyons:

> Les critiques ont toujours difficilement relié les actes de prouesse aux scènes d'amour dans l'*Yvain*. Si la vie chevaleresque de l'amant de Laudine constitue une sorte d'ascension morale, le poète néanmoins se contente de juxtaposer les faits d'armes et les explications sentimentales. Les actes de prouesse ne donnent au chevalier aucun droit sur le cœur de la dame, du moins dans la scène de réconciliation ... Quand Yvain cherche à rejoindre Laudine, c'est que la séparation le fait souffrir au-delà des limites de l'endurance ... Pour expliquer le pardon de Laudine, Chrétien ne met pas en valeur ici les mérites guerriers du chevalier vainqueur. Seul l'attachement à la dame rend possible la réconciliation des amants et le chevalier, en vrai suppliant de l'amour courtois, ne demande rien qu'à titre de grâce. (*61*, pp.375-76)

May the debate continue, as Chrétien surely intended it to do!

Appendix

Chrétien de Troyes and Bernart de Ventadorn

In *Yvain* Chrétien makes use of many motifs from the poetry of Bernart de Ventadorn whom Topsfield (*84*, p.121) describes as 'an exemplary courtly lover, court poet and courtly play-actor' and 'The first troubadour who uses these courtly commonplaces of love extensively' (p.123). Below I give a selection of such commonplaces with reference to the edition of Bernart by M. Lazar (see *3*).

Lament at the decay of love:
Yv. 18-28   Bern. 5,19-21; 11,1-8,9-16; 36,17-24; 23,9-16.

Improvement through love:
Yv. 2489-92   Bern. 5,39-40; 6,17-18; 11,29; 13,14-15 etc.

Lover's impulsiveness:
Yv. 1302-04   Bern. 20,19-21.

Lovers' 'folie':
Yv. 1305-08, 1323-24   Bern. 13,26-27; 15,31-32; 16,23-24; 28,13-14.

The prison of love:
Yv. 1922-42   Bern. 1,21-22; 36,49-52; 37,45; 39,17-18.

Love descends where it pleases:
Yv. 1395ff.   Bern. 27,25-28.

Fickleness of women:
Yv. 1435ff.   Bern. 17,23-24.

Perversity of women:
Yv. 1640-44   Bern. 31,33-36.

Importance of humility:
Yv. 2014-17   Bern. 7,15-21.

Lover's willingness to be killed by the lady:
Yv. 1979-81   Bern. 38,59-60; 42,74.

The lady will not bite the suitor:
Yv. 1966-67   Bern. 1,55-56.

The lover's fear:
Yv. 1950ff.   Bern. 3,14-16.

The lover loses his tongue:
Yv. 1959-63   Bern. 40,37-40.

Feudal homage of lover to lady:
Yv. 1972-74   Bern. 4,57-58; 7,38-42; 18,46-49;
                       37,39-41.

Lover will return to his lady like a bird:
Yv. 2582-84   Bern. 4,49-52

Bibliography

This list of titles is largely confined to items to which reference is made in the text. For fuller materials consult Douglas Kelly, *Chrétien de Troyes: an analytical bibliography*, Research Bibliographies and Checklists 17 (London, Grant and Cutler, 1976) and Otto Klapp, *Bibliographie der französischen Literaturwissenschaft* 12- (Frankfurt am Main, Klostermann, 1974-).

TEXTS:

1. L. Constans (ed.), *Le Roman de Troie par Benoit de Sainte-Maure*, Société des anciens textes français, t.I-VI (Paris, Firmin-Didot, 1904-12; repr. London/New York, Johnson, 1968).

2. P.F. Dembowski (ed.), *La Vie de Sainte Marie l'Egyptienne: versions en ancien et en moyen français*, Publications romanes et françaises, 144 (Genève, Droz, 1977).

3. M. Lazar (ed.), *Bernart de Ventadour: Chansons d'amour*, Bibliothèque française et romane, série B, vol. 5 (Paris, Klincksieck, 1966).

4. G.E. McCracken (ed. & transl.), *Saint Augustine: The City of God against the Pagans*, vol. 1, The Loeb Classical Library (London, Heinemann, 1967).

5. J.H. Mozley (ed. & transl.), *Ovid: The Art of Love and other poems*, The Loeb Classical Library (London, Heinemann, 1929).

6. J.B. Pike (transl.), *Frivolities of Courtiers and Footprints of Philosophers. Being a translation of the first, second and third books of the 'Policraticus' of John of Salisbury* (Minnesota, 1938; repr. New York, Octagon, 1972).

7. M. Platnauer (ed. & transl.), *Claudian*, vol. II, The Loeb Classical Library (London, Heinemann, 1922) (I have modernized the quotation from p.5).

8. A.R. Press, *Anthology of Troubadour Lyric Poetry* (Edinburgh U.P., 1971).

9. T.B.W. Reid (ed.), *Chrestien de Troyes: Yvain (Le Chevalier au Lion). The critical text of Wendelin Foerster with introduction, notes and glossary* (Manchester U.P., 1942; repr. 1984).

10. H. Rushton Fairclough (ed. & transl.), *Virgil*, vol. II, The Loeb Classical Library (London, Heinemann, 1916) (I have modernized the quotation from p.567).

11. H. Rackham (ed. & transl.), *Pliny: Natural History*, vol. III, The Loeb Classical Library (London, Heinemann, 1940).

12. A.L. Wheeler (ed. & transl.), *Ovid: Tristia, Ex Ponto*, The Loeb Classical Library (London, Heinemann, 1924).

STUDIES:

13. Benton, J.F., 'The court of Champagne as a literary center', *Speculum*, 36 (1961), 551-91.
14. Biller, G., *Etude sur le style des premiers romans français en vers (1150-75)*, Göteborgs Högskolas Årsskrift 1916, iv (Göteborg, 1916).
15. ——, *Remarques sur la syntaxe des groupes de propositions dans les premiers romans français en vers (1150-75)*, Göteborgs Högskolas Årsskrift 1920, i (Göteborg, 1920).
16. Boase, R., *The Origin and Meaning of Courtly Love: a critical study of European scholarship* (Manchester U.P., 1977).
17. Bogdanow, F., 'The tradition of the troubadours and the treatment of the love theme in Chrétien de Troyes' *Chevalier au Lion*', *Arthurian Literature*, 2 (Woodbridge, D.S. Brewer, 1982), 76-91.
18. Boklund, K., 'On the spatial and cultural characteristics of courtly romance', *Semiotica*, 20 (1977), 1-37.
19. Bozóky, E., 'Roman arthurien et conte populaire: les règles de conduite et le héros élu', *Cahiers de civilisation médiévale*, 21 (1978), 31-36.
20. Busby, K., *Gauvain in Old French Literature* (Amsterdam, Rodopi, 1980).
21. Chrétien de Troyes: *Europe*, 642 (Oct. 1982) (various articles, pp.3-137).
22. Cline, R.H., 'Heart and eyes', *Romance Philology*, 25 (1971-72), 263-97.
23. Colby, A.M., *The Portrait in Twelfth-Century Literature: an example of the stylistic originality of Chrétien de Troyes* (Genève, Droz, 1965).
24. Contamine, P., *La Guerre au moyen âge*, Nouvelle Clio, 24 (Paris, P.U.F., 1980) (very full bibliography on pp.11-68).
25. Cooper, H., 'Magic that does not work', *Medievalia et Humanistica*, N.S., 7 (1976), 131-46.
26. Cowdrey, H.E.J., 'The peace and the truce of God in the eleventh century', *Past and Present*, 46 (1970), 42-67.
27. Dällenbach, L., *Le Récit spéculaire: essai sur la mise en abyme* (Paris, Seuil, 1977).
28. Diekamp, C., *Formelhafte Synonymenhäufungen in der altpoitevinischen Urkundensprache, 13.Jahrhundert: Beiträge zu Problemen der Synonymenhäufungen im Altfranzösischen*, Romanica Monacensia, 8 (Munich, Fink, 1972).
29. Duby, G., 'Youth in aristocratic society: northwestern France in the twelfth century', in *id.*, *The Chivalrous Society*, transl. Cynthia Postan (London, Arnold, 1977), pp.112-22.
30. ——, *Medieval Marriage: two models for twelfth-century France*, transl. E. Forster (Baltimore/London, Johns Hopkins U.P., 1978).
31. ——, *Le Chevalier, la femme et le prêtre: le mariage dans la France féodale* (Paris, Hachette, 1981) (Engl. transl. by B. Bray, London, Allen Lane, 1984).

32. Ferrante, J.M., 'The conflict of lyric conventions and romance form', in *eadem et* Economou, G.D. (eds.), *In Pursuit of Perfection: courtly love in medieval literature* (New York/London, Kennikat, 1975), pp.135-78.
33. Frappier, J., 'La Brisure du couplet dans *Erec et Enide*', *Romania*, 86 (1965), 1-21.
34. ——, 'Le motif du 'don contraignant' dans la littérature du moyen âge', *Travaux de linguistique et de littérature publiés par le Centre de philologie et de littératures romanes de l'Université de Strasbourg*, VII, 2, *Etudes littéraires* (1969), pp.7-46, repr. in *id.*, *Amour courtois et Table Ronde* (Genève, Droz, 1973), pp.225-64.
35. ——, *Etude sur Yvain ou le Chevalier au lion de Chrétien de Troyes* (Paris, SEDES, 1969).
36. —— and R.R. Grimm (eds.), *Le Roman jusqu'à la fin du XIIIe siècle*, Grundriss der romanischen Literaturen des Mittelalters, IV/I (Heidelberg, Winter, 1978).
37. Frye, N., *Anatomy of Criticism* (Princeton U.P., 1957).
38. Gallais, P., *Genèse du roman occidental: essais sur Tristan et Iseut et son modèle persan* (Paris, Tête de Feuilles, 1974).
39. Green, D.H., *Irony in the Medieval Romance* (Cambridge U.P., 1979).
40. Grigsby, J.L., 'Narrative voices in Chrétien de Troyes: a prolegomenon to dissection', *Romance Philology*, 32 (1978-79), 261-73.
41. Grimbert, J.T., 'Adversative structure in Chrétien's *Yvain*: the role of the conjunction *mes*', *Medioevo Romanzo*, 9 (1984), 27-50.
42. Gruber, J., *Die Dialektik des Trobar. Untersuchungen zur Struktur und Entwicklung des occitanischen und französischen Minnesangs des 12.Jahrhunderts*, Beihefte zur Zeitschrift für romanische Philologie, 194 (Tübingen, Niemeyer, 1983).
43. Haidu, P., *Lion-queue-coupée: l'écart symbolique chez Chrétien de Troyes*, Histoire des idées et critique littéraire, 123 (Genève, Droz, 1972).
44. Halligan, G.J., 'Marriage in Chrétien's *Yvain*', *AUMLA*, 34 (1970), 264-85.
45. Hanning, R.W., *The Individual in Twelfth-Century Romance* (New Haven, Yale U.P., 1977).
46. Harnack, A., *Militia Christi: the Christian religion and the military in the first three centuries*, translated and introduced by David McInnes Gracie (Philadelphia, Fortress Press, 1981).
47. Heffernan, C.F., 'Chrétien de Troyes's *Yvain*: seeking the fountain', *Res Publica Litterarum*, 5 (1982), 109-21.
48. Hume, K., 'Romance: a perdurable pattern', *College English*, 36 (1974), 129-46.
49. Hunt, T., 'The rhetorical background to the Arthurian prologue: tradition and the Old French vernacular prologues', *Forum for Modern Language Studies*, 6 (1970), 1-23.
50. ——, 'Tradition and originality in the prologues of Chrestien de Troyes', *ibid.*, 8 (1972), 320-44.

51. ——, 'Glossing Marie de France', *Romanische Forschungen*, 86 (1974), 396-418.

52. ——, 'The dialectic of *Yvain*', *Modern Language Review*, 72 (1977), 285-99.

53. ——, 'Chrestien and the Latin *comediae*', *Mediaeval Studies*, 40 (1978), 120-56.

54. ——, 'The emergence of the knight in France and England, 1000-1200', *Forum for Modern Language Studies*, 17 (1981), 93-114, repr. in W.H. Jackson (ed.), *Knighthood in Medieval Literature* (Woodbridge, D.S. Brewer, 1981), pp.1-22.

55. ——, 'The medieval adaptations of Chrétien's *Yvain*: a bibliographical essay' in K. Varty (ed.), *An Arthurian Tapestry: essays in memory of Lewis Thorpe* (Glasgow, 1981), pp.203-13.

56. ——, 'Chrétien de Troyes' Arthurian Romance, *Yvain*' in B. Ford (ed.), *The New Pelican Guide to English Literature*, vol.1, pt.2. *Medieval Literature: The European Inheritance* (Harmondsworth, Penguin, 1983), pp.126-41.

57. ——, 'The Lion and Yvain', in P.B. Grout *et al.* (eds.), *The Legend of Arthur in the Middle Ages: studies presented to A.H. Diverres by colleagues, pupils and friends*, Arthurian Studies, 7 (Woodbridge, D.S. Brewer, 1983), pp.86-98, 237-40.

58. Jonin, P., 'Le Vasselage de Lancelot dans le *Conte de la charrette*', *Le Moyen Age*, 58 (1952), 281-98.

59. Lefay-Toury, M.-N., 'Roman breton et mythe courtois: l'évolution du personnage féminin dans les romans de Chrétien de Troyes', *Cahiers de civilisation médiévale*, 15 (1972), 193-204, 283-93.

60. Luttrell, C., *The Creation of the First Arthurian Romance: a quest* (London, Arnold, 1974).

61. Lyons, F., 'Sentiment et rhétorique dans l'*Yvain*', *Romania*, 83 (1962), 370-77.

62. McCash, J.H.M., 'Marie de Champagne and Eleanor of Aquitaine: a relationship re-examined', *Speculum*, 54 (1979), 698-711.

63. Ménard, P., 'Le don en blanc qui lie le donateur: réflexions sur un motif de conte' in *An Arthurian Tapestry* (see above, *55*), pp.37-53.

64. Morris, C., *The Discovery of the Individual, 1050-1200* (London, S.P.C.K., 1972).

65. Noble, P.S., *Love and Marriage in Chrétien de Troyes* (Cardiff, Univ. of Wales Press, 1982).

66. Nordahl, H., 'Figure rhétorique, rhétorisabilité et rhétorisation: quelques réflexions sur les tautologies binaires en ancien français', *Zeitschrift für französische Sprache und Literatur*, 92 (1982), 124-31.

67. Ourliac, P., 'Troubadours et juristes', *Cahiers de civilisation médiévale*, 8 (1965), 159-77.

68. Payen, J.C., & F.N.M. Diekstra *et al.*, *Le Roman*, Typologie des sources du moyen âge occidental, fasc. 12 (Turnhout, Brepols, 1975).

69. Pelan, M., 'Old French *s'oublier*; its meaning in epic and courtly literature', *Romanistisches Jahrbuch*, 10 (1959), 59-77.

70. Philipot, E., 'Le Roman du *Chevalier au lion* de Chrestien de Troyes (étude littéraire)', *Annales de Bretagne*, 8 (1892-93), 33-83, 321-45, 455-79.

71. Piehler, P., *The Visionary Landscape* (London, Arnold, 1971).

72. Press, A.R., 'The adulterous nature of *fin' amors*: a re-examination of the theory', *Forum for Modern Language Studies*, 6 (1970), 327-41.

73. ——, 'Chrétien de Troyes's Laudine: a Belle Dame sans Mercy', *Forum for Modern Language Studies*, 19 (1983), 158-71.

74. Russell, F.H., *The Just War in the Middle Ages* (Cambridge U.P., 1975).

75. Schmolke-Hasselmann, B., *Der arthurische Versroman von Chrétien bis Froissart: zur Geschichte einer Gattung*, Beihefte zur Zeitschrift für romanische Philologie, 177 (Tübingen, Niemeyer, 1980).

76. Schnell, R., 'Von der kanonistischen zur höfischen Ehekasuistik: Gautiers d'Arras *Ille et Galeron*', *Zeitschrift für romanische Philologie*, 98 (1982), 257-95.

77. Scholz, M.G., *Hören und lesen: Studien zur primären Rezeption der Literatur im 12. und 13.Jahrhundert* (Wiesbaden, Steiner, 1980).

78. Shirt, D.J., '*Cligés*: a twelfth-century matrimonial case book?', *Forum for Modern Language Studies*, 18 (1982), 75-89.

79. Stanger, M.D., 'Literary patronage at the medieval court of Flanders', *French Studies*, 11 (1957), 214-29.

80. Stefenelli, A., 'Lexikalische Variatio in Chrétiens *Yvain*', *Zeitschrift für romanische Philologie*, 81 (1965), 250-87.

81. Stevens, J., *Medieval Romance: themes and approaches* (London, Hutchinson, 1973).

82. Stock, B., *The Implications of Literacy: written language and models of interpretation in the eleventh and twelfth centuries* (Princeton U.P., 1982).

83. Thoss, D., *Studien zum 'locus amoenus' im Mittelalter* (Wien, Braumüller, 1972).

84. Topsfield, L.T., *Troubadours and Love* (Cambridge U.P., 1975).

85. ——, *Chrétien de Troyes: a study of the Arthurian romances* (Cambridge U.P., 1981).

86. Vinaver, E., *The Rise of Romance* (Oxford U.P., 1971; repr. Woodbridge, D.S. Brewer, 1984).

87. Vogel, I., *Die affektive Intensivierung der adjektiva mit Hilfe des Vergleichs im Altfranzösischen*, Studia Romanica, 12 (Heidelberg, Winter, 1967).

88. Wetherbee, W., *Platonism and Poetry in the Twelfth Century* (Princeton U.P., 1972).

89. Zai, M.-C., *Les Chansons courtoises de Chrétien de Troyes: édition critique, avec introduction, notes et commentaire*, Publications

universitaires européennes, série XIII, vol.27 (Berne/Francfort/M., Lang, 1974).

90. Ziltener, W., *Studien zur bildungsgeschichtlichen Eigenart der höfischen Dichtung: Antike und Christentum in okzitanischen und altfranzösischen Vergleichen aus der unbelebten Natur*, Romanica Helvetica, 83 (Berne, Francke, 1972).

91. ——, *Repertorium der Gleichnisse und bildhaften Vergleiche der okzitanischen und der französischen Versliteratur des Mittelalters*, Heft 1- (Berne, Francke, 1972-).

CRITICAL GUIDES TO FRENCH TEXTS

edited by
Roger Little, Wolfgang van Emden, David Williams